HEALING *of a* PSYCHOTHERAPIST:

A Story of Rebellion, Reflection, and Redemption

Charles C. McCormack

First Published as Essense in 2021

ISBN 9798218196394

charlesmccormack81@gmail.com

Dedication:

Chandler, Keeley, and Cait.
Who taught me what love is,

And Janet,
Who taught me what love does.

TABLE *of* CONTENTS

Epitaph

Be who you is, cuz if you be what you ain't, then you ain't what you is.

Gravestone epitaph, Boot hill Cemetery, Tombstone, AZ

Prologue

Essence, the original title of ***Healing of a Psychotherapist***, is the story of a Hero's Journey. The noun Hero is used here in the spirit of Joseph Cambell's work: *The Hero with a Thousand Faces*. Campbell's title conveys that every person is on a Hero's journey, challenged ever-more to become themselves, to strip down to their essence. Of course, some reject the venture, and others fail. Still, others succeed, though never without reversals, as they blaze the trail of their lives. In writing Essence, I had not expected such a challenging and illuminating process, resulting in letting go of many conceits and the discovery that doing so was not a loss but a gain, an unburdening that lightened my spirit.

Now, as I stand here, looking out upon the Bush River, bejeweled in the rust, copper, and gold leaves of fall, I wonder what you will think, for this story requires I reveal the soft underbelly of this writer, often in ways that are less than appealing. But, to stay true to myself, I must walk my talk from shadowed worlds to sunlit landscapes.

My daughter Keeley and my son Chandler inspired this book. Years ago, Keeley gave me a book of questions for grandparents to express who they were for posterity. The idea appealed, but the structure did not. Separately, Chandler asked what I thought it [life] was about. His work and home life were going well, and he wondered, "Is this it?" On the spur of the moment, and from somewhere deep within, I answered, "It's about the pursuit of happiness."

Chandler didn't seem convinced. My reflexive answer was neither articulate nor compelling. From that day on, I felt a need to make my case.

I translated Keeley and Chandler's challenges into two questions: "Who am I?" and "What's it all about?" As I relived my life from the Gathering Darkness of my early years, through the directionless acting out of my teens, into my twenties, where I began to find myself, and finally arriving at a state of partial fulfillment today, I recognized that my story was unique to me, but the struggle was not. I became painfully aware of how deeply the troubled times in my life had shaped me in previously unarticulated ways and how confronting their impact upon me was strikingly beneficial in lessening their ability to impede my efforts to be happy.

To tell this story, I must throw caution to the wind and lay bare all the layers of uncertainty, shame, low self-esteem, egotism, mistakes made and then made again, the lessons learned and then forgotten, the failures and successes, the joys and heartbreaks, and the wisdom and folly that constricted me like the successive shells of a Russian Nesting Doll.

Reconciling the disparate parts of ourselves is not easy. We naturally recoil from psychological pain and emotional discomfort. Nonetheless, the price of not doing so is high, for repression is not a surgical instrument but a sledgehammer; it does not curtail single undesired thoughts or feelings but rather the capacity to think and feel in general. Inevitably, avoidance and denial make us deaf, dumb, and numb to ourselves. When we deny our afflictions, baser impulses, or feelings, we hinder our capacity to think and feel in general, including the ability to drink in the colors of a beautiful sunset or the confounding bliss of a tender kiss. The paradox of psychological health is that it entails feeling *more of everything*, both the pleasurable and the painful, not less. It is an elixir of a curse and a blessing in one vial.

Notably, the cost of avoidance does not end with a deadening in our capacity to feel. Although pushed from awareness, the edited thoughts, feelings, and memories are not gone. Rather, what begins as gathering darkness in the creosote recesses of our minds becomes an ever-growing disquiet as we relegate more and more to their number. Inevitably and insidiously, the banished begin leaking out in disguised and twisted ways, manifesting in various forms, such as inexplicable anger or sorrow, hostility, depression, anxiety, dread, emptiness, and somatic complaints. We carry these symptoms with us wherever we go, first as a general unease but eventually swelling into bells of alarm, all the more disquieting because the cause eludes us.

For sure, experiencing *all* our feelings and thinking *all* our thoughts is not always a happy business. Life and relationships can be scary and embarrassing. Confronting our losses and less than socially acceptable thoughts and behaviors can be destabilizing because doing so does not always support the socially valued semblance of a tidy life. However, grappling with our issues increases our capacity to think and feel and the opportunity to become more self-accepting and self-assured, establishing a self-relationship founded in the terra firma of reality rather than the quick-sand of ego-driven stories and self-delusions. Indeed, regardless of how tarnished we humans can be, I propose that the difficult path of feeling both the good and the bad of our imperfect state to reconcile ourselves with it *is* the path to a happier and more meaningful life.

Awareness of the dark side of the human condition is ancient. In Cherokee lore, the Chieftain tells his grandson the story of the two wolves. He says, "Within me, two wolves are constantly at war. One, the Evil Wolf, feeds on anger, envy, sorrow, greed, arrogance, self-pity, resentment, inferiority, false pride, superiority, and ego. The other, the Good Wolf, feeds on joy, love, serenity, humility, kindness, benevolence, empathy, truth, compassion, and faith." Tenderly looking into his grandson's eyes, the Chieftain says, "You have these two wolves in you as well. Everyone has them." The grandson, face furrowed by thought, considers this. Then, eyes widening with anticipation, he asks his grandfather, "Which one wins?" Laughing, the grandfather leans forward and whispers, "Whichever one you feed."

Cherokee Indians are not alone in speaking of the dark side of man. The psychoanalyst, Carl Jung, called it the Shadow and warned that one either digests his shadow or the shadow will digest him. Melanie Klein, who pioneered the analysis of children, asserted that the feelings of love, hate, jealousy, greed, lust, and envy are all part of being human and warns that the effort to deny these feelings, rather than to understand them, is self-rejecting and destructive. Freud spoke of the Id as that part of the psyche that houses primitive impulses and posited that these fuel creativity and destructiveness. He asserted that these impulses must be integrated, not eliminated, to live successfully in society.

Whatever the theory, the point is that from the earliest age, while the human brain is in the nascence of its development, there is a Gathering Darkness, a distillation of painful experiences from which none of us are free. Whatever we call it, the Evil Wolf, the Shadow, the Id, or even original sin, it is natural and alive within us: it is part of us. And, if we deny its existence, it only clamors ever more loudly to be heard.

It is essential to realize that these dire predictions prove prophetic no matter how much we flourish in the external world. We all have heard of many famous and wildly successful people who have succumbed to depression, drug addiction, or suicide, thus confirming that fame and fortunes protect no man from his demons: The Evil Wolf ignored bites ever harder.

Please be aware that mine is not a story of rising from material impoverishment. Far from it, I was always well-fed, housed, and clothed; my family was middle to upper-middle class. Mine was a different kind of impoverishment, one of not being able to count on the people in charge of my life to keep me safe, to provide the stability and reliability necessary to form basic trust and optimism, the foundational pillars of a happy person. Instead, the early, relentless breaches in security rendered me forever vigilant; part of my brain was always at work trying to anticipate and ward off the next upset that was "sure" to arise, thus hindering my ability to relax and fully enjoy the moment.

The title, *Healing of a Psychotherapist,* represents my ongoing struggle to extricate myself from these early lessons in service of becoming more fully myself. It recounts my attempts to reconcile with the dark side of my external world and the inner world of my psyche. In so doing, I gradually broke through the self-limiting *lessons* of my childhood that only constrained me, limiting my happiness and my imagining of who I could be.

Everyone has an engaging story to tell but usually does not realize it. Here, the story of the three fish helps to illustrate this. Two fish are swimming one way as a third swims the other. In passing, the single fish calls out, "Hello. How's the water today?" Once past, the pair of fish look at each other, and one puts his puzzlement to words, "What's water?" I've spent a lifetime trying to discover the unseen waters of my life and helping others do the same with theirs.

Interestingly, research suggests that the ability to remember our history affects our capacity to imagine alternative futures. Fortunately, once we begin remembering, other memories tumble out, deepening our understanding of how we came to be the way we are and offering the choice of changing our lives or not. The decision is solely ours to make. The important thing is to symbolize our experience, to represent it in some way, such as in words, dance, music, or art—for thinking is a symbolic process, and without thought, we are deaf and dumb to ourselves.

Please be aware that I do not mean to suggest that biology does not play a part in our capacity for happiness. Countless people suffer from biologically driven mental disorders, including anxiety and depression. Nonetheless, while I have seen many people become stabilized with the help of medication and psychotherapy, I have never seen anyone develop a fulfilling life who did not assume personal responsibility for it.

Lastly, please understand that this is my version of events. Perception and memory are notoriously malleable. Parts of my story will agree with those who have lived alongside me, while others will differ. I have no qualms about this. We can each have our *truth* as long as we leave room for the truths of others.

PART I

A GATHERING DARKNESS

The psyche is like a tree trunk, early experience forever imprinted on the tender flesh of the inner rings. It is the inner rings upon which all else rests, confirming William Wordsworth's assertion that "The child is the father of the man." Amazing—a critical time of life, yet before and beyond words.

CHAPTER 1

Dad: Violence and Belittling

"Charlie, fetch me a martini! Charlie, polish my boots. Charlie, come with me; I'm going to the store. Dammit, Charlie, get over here when I call you." The sound of his voice was a whiplash, never brooking dissent: commanding, demanding, relentless and unforgiving. I had to get away, but where could I go?

I grew up in two families: one when my father, John McCormack, an artillery officer of Irish descent, was there, the other when he was not. The family of my father's teachings was tyrannical and sadistic, interspersed with hypo-manic moments of humor fueled by the tensions and anxieties that had preceded it.

Born to a prominent Memphis, Tennessee, family that boasted black servants and field hands and a distinguished history of military service, Dad was of devout Southern traditions and beliefs. Famously, his father was an aid to General Black Jack Pershing and his mother, a Washington D. C. socialite. With this ballyhooed heritage, Dad touted military values of honor and bravery, yet his day-to-day actions were those of a spoiled child.

What Dad valued were not the human capacities to think or feel, to be curious, or to question, but the machine-like ability to "Do what you're told, when you're told." Any questioning was equated with "back talk" and quickly earned a hefty slap.

Dad fancied himself another General Douglas MacArthur. "Get in line," he would command, and my siblings and I would stand in a line. "Put your hands behind your backs," and like soldiers at parade rest, we would clasp our hands behind our backs. Of course, this put us in a vulnerable position for whatever was to come. Then he would harangue us with our inadequacies for whatever we had or had not done, real or imagined.

One time, we had come home late for dinner, having lost track of time in play. Dad started his rant, "You are all ins-s-sufferable, s-s-s-selfish little shits, behaving like f-f-f-fools. Have you no-o-o care for a-a-anyo-o-o-one else? Your m-m-mother was worried, and you held dinner up." To my accounting, mother had not seemed at all worried. I knew Dad was just seeking a ready receptacle in which to discharge his alcohol-fueled aggression.

Of course, his stutter made it difficult for him to pull off the commanding persona. After all, it is hard to sell a commanding persona when face straining and going through shades of red and blue, you are strangling on your own words.

We all stood there silently, watching him wrestle with himself, waiting for what we knew was to come: stinging slaps to the face while we kept our hands locked together behind our backs. There was a shaming in all this, forcing us to become unwilling collaborators in the assault on ourselves. Somehow, I managed to translate this into a kind of heroic deed: I tell myself I can take it and refuse to whimper or complain. I would not give him the pleasure of that.

Strangely, I grew to welcome the slaps as they typically signaled the culmination of his bullying and the dreadful experience of watching his face contort and turn beetroot as he struggled mightily to push his words up his throat and out his mouth. The one thing I learned: if there is no avoiding a slap, get it over with.

He continued, "You not only disres-res-res—"

"Disrespect?" I blurted out.

Unable to bear the gruesome sight a second longer, I would impulsively offer a word upon which he was foundering in the hopes of speeding the seemingly endless ordeal to its end.

I guessed correctly.

"You also disgrace your mother and l-l-l—"

"Leave?"

Wrong, this time. My unfortunate impulse to hurry things along when mistaken only added to the growing volcano of dad's frustrations, escalating the feeling of chaos and *d-d-d-dread.*

His face turned purple, and he stepped forward and slapped me, always the face.

It stung, but I had gotten used to the sensation.

"Get out of my sight. Tomorrow you're grounded," which meant we would be working for dad all day. Given the hours-long proximity to him the grounding entailed, and the apprehension I felt when in his presence, this was a far worse fate than the slapping itself.

Dad idolized courage in fighting, telling heroic tales of his ancestors and his battlefield accomplishments rivaling the Legends of Daniel Boone, Jim Bowie, and Davy Crockett. Sometimes, he would recount a story of me as a child, swarmed in a scrum of kids, only to rise pugnaciously undaunted out of the melee. I do not recall this event, but the story drove home the point: If you want to be worth anything, never give up.

Such an attitude sounds admirable, yet it could be problematic. Sometimes it is wise to give up, especially if you, like me, are not a good fighter. I can honestly say I have never won a fight. I have, however, taken a severe and conclusive beating only to have my assailant quit for fear of killing me.

For all his intellect, Dad was strangely devoid of compassion. Perhaps the worst thing about my dad was that he was callous of heart. Once, he shoved puppies into a bag and tossed them into the lake, proudly proclaiming that he was preserving the bloodlines of his hunting dogs. His lack of empathy for them was mind-bending. How much would it take to imagine what those puppies went through? The pain and terror they felt being stuffed into the dark and claustrophobic confines of a burlap bag, the disorientation of becoming weightless as they were tossed into the air, then the fighting and clawing to escape as they splashed into the lake, cold water pouring in from all sides, panicking to the very end until the cruel death took them.

Another of my father's dubious achievements occurred when we had been hunting. More accurately, Dad had been hunting; the kids dragged along to keep him company. Nestled in thorny bushes from morning to early afternoon, with nothing but withering scrubs and sweltering heat to bear, Dad mercifully announced he was ready to leave. Parched and pummeled by the sun, which is all I wanted. So, it was my utter frustration when, at the last minute, Dad spotted a hawk silhouetted majestically on a treetop upon a distant hill. Having found a target, particularly one so gloriously poised, he had to take the shot. I hated him for that. My heart opened to the hawk, which, though fully present to its moment, was oblivious to the looming danger. I understood what it did not: It had seen the last of its moments. I railed in my mind, *What's the point?* But I had no say.

The report of the rifle startled me. But surprisingly, the hawk remained perched upon its tree and then, to my delight, took flight. A happy yelp, charged with the joy of the bird's escape and my father's loss of his ill-imagined glory, escaped my lips. It was a premature indulgence that was short-lived. Standing despondently under the glow of the sun, I stared in shock as the bird crumpled in on itself and plummeted to the ground like an old work glove, a husk of the noble predator it had once been. I had been fooled. The bird had not taken flight but was lifted in the air by a bullet that took a couple of seconds longer than I had expected to traverse its course. Bile filled my heart where joy had been, and a mist of melancholy settled upon me: there was no escaping.

The truly appalling aspect of this was that Dad had inflicted the hawk's death as easily as snapping one's fingers and with even lesser concern. The bald-faced shamelessness of this act was only compounded when Dad cautioned us not to say a thing, explaining that hawks were on the protected species list. There was no suggestion of moral or ethical conflict; the only concern was getting caught.

I do not want to suggest that it was always unhappy when Dad was around. When he was in a good mood, we all breathed more easily and rode the coattails of his gregariousness. I always looked forward to Sundays, when he traditionally cooked enormous breakfasts, suffusing the house with aromas of corn beef hash, grits, fried eggs, bacon, and French toast.

And he could surprise me, unexpectedly exhibiting talents I had not known he possessed. One sunny afternoon, he took us to a farm. In the yard was a stallion, a prancing beast bristling with raw power. Its corded muscles moved like writhing snakes beneath its glistening black coat.

Alongside it, Dad, dressed in his riding garb, a riding crop in hand, dark hair slicked back from his high forehead, and spit-shined riding boots reflecting the sun, cut a dashing figure.

I stood in frightened awe as Dad mounted the beast. To my amazement, Dad, unperturbed, controlled the horse with ease and spurred the stallion into a breakaway run, rider and horse melding together as they disappeared across the meadow. Until that moment, I had no idea he could ride a horse, let alone a terrifying one.

For my part, I felt that if love was slow in being returned, it must be because of me. Years later, I wanted to test my ability to make him happy. I bought him a special Christmas gift that year that outshone the one I had gotten mother—a complete reversal of the usual course of things. I bought him a gold golf tee, a golf hat bedecked with ornaments sure to garner humorous attention on the links, and a new pair of golf shoes. I was not with them that Christmas, but Mother, full of mirth, phoned saying, "Charlie, you've created a monster. Your dad is walking all over the house in his golf shoes." I was pleased to have been able to make him happy. However, he never acknowledged the gift nor thanked me. I would later understand that generosity of spirit and the capacity for heartfelt gratitude are two sides of the same coin; a coin Dad did not possess.

CHAPTER 2

Mom: Imperfect Love

Happily, when Dad was not around, we were in the family of Madeleine Turgeon McCormack, later nicknamed Mutti (German for mother). Mutti created a warm and happy environment. We were secure in her love and the knowledge she would never do us harm—or so I believed. In Mutti's family, it was not all about her; it was about the kids, and I transformed from a worthless cog to the valued second born of four brothers and one sister: Jacques, me, Edward, Mark, and Michelle.

Mom was a French Canadian, born and raised in Quebec to a wealthy lumber family; English was her second language. Her cousin, Roger

Lemelin, authored four novels and wrote and produced a TV series in Canada. He won the Legion d'Honneur for his contribution to Canadian culture and a Prix David for a book entitled *The Town Below*, partly based on his observations of my mother's family, who lived in the celebrated Upper Town. Mother's brother, George, a Kennedy-esque figure, was a millionaire. He founded and then sold a frozen meat pie company and spent his time skiing or sailing in the South of France.

But not all had been well in Mutti's family: One brother accidentally hung himself at the age of six while playing cowboys and Indians. Her mother, Matilde, was repeatedly hospitalized for depression, and her father, a lumber baron and an alcoholic, went bankrupt and missed her wedding due to a hangover. The last child living at home, Guy, was taken away by social services.

Mutti was strong; she had to be. While my father was away during the Korean War, on maneuvers, or transferred from one posting to the next, she was raising five kids. As he went ahead, she followed behind, tasked with closing the old house and transitioning to the new one. Her job was homemaker, and my father's was to be an army officer. He never helped around the house and was, in fact, more a burden than a blessing, repeatedly calling my mother or one of the kids to wait on him in petty ways.

I still hear his voice grating on my ears, "Charlie! Bring me a martini," or, "Charlie! Come here. Turn on that light," the lamp infuriatingly well within his reach.

The curious thing was that he thought nothing of this kingly behavior, childish too, nor did Mutti. To them, his maddening sense of entitlement was the most natural thing in the world. In this, they were like pieces of broken glass fitting perfectly together.

Their early marriage seemed satisfactory, but as the years passed and the children grew older, so did the parental conflict. Sometimes, Mutti, out of a mother's love and to divert him from an excessively abusive episode with the kids, would speak to him in castrating tones, seeming to hunger for a fight, egging him on far beyond caution's call. Then, she would be the one to receive the hit and still refuse to back away, playing her part in the ever-repeating cycle of abuse.

As upsetting and divisive as this behavior was, another facet of my parents joined them: They loved to entertain. Christmas and Thanksgiving were always sparkling events, the house alive with well-dressed people and the buzz of animated conversation as wine-filled crystal glasses splashed their ruby light, and music frolicked out of the top-of-the-line sound system—all serving to create the song of people having a genuinely good time. Upon such occasions, I felt pride in my parents as they each moved around the room with elegance and grace

Mom and Dad were opposites. Mutti was genuinely interested in people and concerned about them. While Dad focused on himself, she focused on others. Many years later, as she was losing her second fight with cancer, she was still all about others, especially Dad. Fighting nausea and fatigue, she ramrodded a move to Aiken, SC, so that Dad would be near Mark and his wife Carol Ann, devout people themselves when she passed.

Yet, despite all the good things about Mutti, two thorns of memory have stuck with me over the decades. In the first, I am age eight, playing in the honeysuckle-scented backyard in Montgomery, Alabama, when I feel an unexpected urge to connect with her. I clamber up the worn wooden steps to the kitchen, enter through the screen door, and find her cooking at the stove, her back to me. I reach out to touch the hem of her skirt when apprehension stills my hand. Unaccountably, I feel vulnerable and fearful of rebuke. Hesitating, I struggle to understand these feelings, pulled in one direction by desire, and pushed in the other by unease. I broke the mounting tension of my impasse by silently leaving the kitchen; Mutti never knew I was there.

This experience suggests that I felt unsafe being vulnerable or needy with my mother, but I could not put the why of it into words. I had cried or shared troubled feelings with her and been comforted. But this was different. I felt fine, just wanting tenderness for tenderness's sake and fearing rejection. I sensed a distinction between my mother being responsive to my anguish versus being sensitive to me. I dreaded rebuke if

I diverted her from her chores without a pressing need, an outcome I was unwilling to risk given the tenderness of my feelings.

In turning away from my mother, I fed the Evil Wolf, succumbing to my fear-ridden imaginings rather than allowing my mother to respond in whatever way she would. In so doing, I remained safe but forfeited any possibility of fulfillment. In such ways, I was to learn that pursuing happiness and fulfillment takes courage, not because it is risk-free, but because it is not.

Years later, when I realized my mother couldn't relate to my feeling of profound loneliness during my separation and divorce from Jane, and after I had learned more about her painful upbringing (of which she never spoke), I suspected that the apprehension I felt all those years earlier had not been entirely misplaced. I wondered what lessons she had drawn from her troubled childhood to protect herself from emotional pain that subsequently interfered with her ability to relate to mine.

However, my apprehension may have also been fueled by the nature of the second memory, which demonstrates a characteristic of my mother that contributed to both her enormous strength and her greatest weakness: her tendency to compartmentalize. In her early years, once she held a belief, it was unshakeable, evidenced not only in the way she loved but also hated in equal measure.

Compartmentalizing was especially evident in her relationship with my stepbrother, Cris, five years older than me, and the product of my father's first marriage. Cris was a *Mad Magazine* (a comic book of the day) caricature of my father. Not only did he try to emulate Dad's behavior, but he also looked like him, albeit in a strangely asymmetrical way: skinny as a blade of grass, bird-eyed, shrunken-chested, and sporting a large head with a receding hairline mirroring Dad's own.

Mother hated him; there was no gentle way to put it. Perhaps some of it was due to his being from Dad's previous marriage. Still, he seemed to create trouble wherever he went, constantly misbehaving in attention-seeking ways, to my mother's mortification.

The thorn of memory I wish to speak of occurred on a sunny summer day in Montgomery, Alabama when I was eight years old.

A kiddy pool was in the backyard, directly under a tree. Cris, thirteen, bare-chested, ribs sticking out, and baggy shorts hanging limply from his non-existent hips, had stepped into the pool and muddied the water.

Mutti noticed from the kitchen window and shouted furiously, "Get out of the pool and stay out. You are not a child."

Cris then opted to climb the tree and literally out on a limb. At first, it was a slapstick moment as the law of gravity showed no mercy; the limb began to bend, tilting Cris upside-down. Eyes bulging, head dangling ludicrously below his legs, and just above the pool surface, we were all laughing uproariously when, with a sharp crack, the branch broke, and it and Cris fell as one into the pool.

Drawn by the electric excitement of our raillery, Mutti looked out the window. She was apoplectic and began screaming at Cris uncontrollably. Unhinged and out for blood, Dad immediately received the pent-up fury of her wrath upon his arrival home from work.

"John, your awful son directly disobeyed me. He muddied the baby pool and then broke a tree limb into the pool. I have had it with him, and you must do something about it! What kind of man are you that you can't control your son?"

To appease her, Dad took Cris upstairs to the main bedroom with its four-poster bed. I snuck along behind to see what was happening.

The eerie quiet filled me with foreboding. Peeking through the door, a premonition of the impending horror to follow filled me with dread. Given Dad's calloused heart, I knew something terrible was about to happen. Dad gruffly ordered, "Cris, take off your clothes except for your underwear." Cris, silently stripped to his underwear.

Dad ordered, "Hold on to the top of the bedpost." Cris complied, thus fully exposing his bony torso, defenseless against whatever was to come.

Slowly, Dad took off his belt, the room so quiet I could hear the belt sliding through the loops of his pants. Then, ominously, with a moment of hesitation that only increased the agony of dread I was feeling, Dad began striking Cris from head to toe and back again, over and over. Aside from Dad's grunting with effort, there was no sound other than the whooshing of the belt and the sickening unforgiving whip-like crack of leather against flesh.

I was sickened but unable to move, frozen in horror and fascination. Finally, afraid of my father's wrath if he should discover me there, I crept away as the sounds of the lashing followed me down the stairway.

Cris, ever desperate for my father's approval, striving to be the brave soldier, refusing to cry out as with eyes squeezed shut and face knotted in agony, silent tears fell upon his concave chest.

Unfortunately, Dad's approval was always in short supply. But for Cris, it was worse: the rest of us had Mutti, while Cris, a confused, proud, and mismatched boy, had no one. That was the unseen water of his life.

The lesson that I learned that day? When such behaviors are perpetuated by those who are supposed to keep us safe, no one is ever truly safe.

In the following years, Cris, exiled from our house and lives, turned to drugs and worked various jobs, finally settling into road work. Cris married, had two kids, and divorced. Occasionally, he would visit Dad, once showing up on a motorcycle, wearing gang colors, with a friend named Spike. In the driveway, he brandished a long-barreled 45-caliber revolver that he extolled as a collector's piece. My mother hissed, "John, get rid of him!" With only ice in his voice, Dad told Cris never to return.

In the years to follow, perhaps sensing my empathy, Cris would visit me on rare occasions. These meetings were always awkward as he continued to be a parody of my father, engaging in self-aggrandizing stories and acts of social inappropriateness that only made me sorry to be with him. Even so, I never told him to go away, and I never told him not to return. I just could not.

Like our paternal grandfather, Cris died in his early fifties from a heart attack. I had not seen him for years. His ex-wife (whom I met only once) and children have no relationship with the rest of the McCormack clan.

As you can see, Mother had her low-light reels. By all accounts, a religious and loving woman, she was still the one who triggered this merciless assault upon Cris; Dad had only done her dirty work. I took in the brutality of that beating and all that led up to it: Cris' desperate need for attention, the unforeseen breaking of the tree limb, my mother's murderous rage, and my father's subservient going along with it.

These experiences taught me that we are all flawed. But even more so: the most dangerous people are those who refuse to see the flaws within themselves.

An emotionally chaotic and violent environment promotes insecurity, mistrust, shame, and doubt. Of course, when you are living through it, you are unaware of the causes of such things or that there is even any such thing as a cause. To the child, everything within the family is "normal"—just the way things are, becoming the unseen water of our lives. Maybe this explains why I developed the self-soothing behaviors of headbanging and nail-biting as a child.

As the saying goes, "When you grow up in a blue world, you don't know the color blue." I can tell you with certainty that when you grow up in gathering darkness, there are few colors at all.

CHAPTER 3

Power and Intimidation: Racism

My memory is far from a continuous thing. It does not lend itself to weaving a seamless story with a beginning, middle, and end. Instead, it consists of snippets of my life that arise unbidden, like shards of glass, and are often equally cutting.

The memory I am about to relate is of that nature, speaking to an ever-present tincture of dread and an abiding potential for violence that mirrored in the outside world what was occurring within my family. Under the glaze of a social veneer, the external threat was often less visible but served to intimidate anyone unwise enough to step outside the cultural norm. This threat is ever more potent because a code of silence surrounds it, and though felt, and its source is difficult to find because of its ubiquity.

I was nine years old on that summer day in 1958, laboring under the searing heat of the Alabama sun as I trudged along a dirt track through what was then known as the colored shantytown. The shacks, ramshackle hovels of gray, aging wood, buckling tin roofs, and tilting wooden porches seemed ready to be swept away in the first crackling winds of a thunderstorm. Though only a few hundred yards from my home, on the other side of the two-lane road, the shantytown was a world apart.

Curiosity had brought me here, like a tourist exploring the spellbinding unfamiliarity of a Third World country.

As I moved deeper into this strange world, mine receded. Thus, untethered, I slogged along, breathing in the reddish clay dust from the path as the aroma of fried chicken and collard greens, cooking in the shadow-worlds beyond torn screen doors, ignited hunger in my belly. Muscular black men in sweat-stained wifebeater t-shirts congregated in twos and threes as the discordant sounds of angry shouts and laughter punctuated the soupy afternoon air. To my unease, these men stared coldly or turned away—none spoke or otherwise acknowledged my presence.

I did not understand this current of hostility. Had I done something? Or was I misreading the situation? Driven by curiosity, I returned several days later, thinking *Maybe I got it wrong*. Inexplicably, it felt important to know. Now, like seeing a movie or reading a book for the second time, I could discern more as I now took note of many downcast faces and the sullenness on the faces of others as they looked away. Particularly striking was that despite such potent silent communication, none dared to speak. I then realized that the hostility was real and more so that fear and anxiety lurked beneath it. Although I did not understand the cause, I sensed that I somehow represented a danger to these people and that my presence upset them. I never intruded into their world again.

The first time I went to the movies in Montgomery, I noticed that the "coloreds" got to sit on the balcony while the whites sat on the ground floor. I was annoyed: *Why do they get the best seats?* To me, sitting up high was a lot more fun than sitting below. Only dimly did I recognize that the whites and coloreds sat apart, something I later learned was called "segregation."

After the movie, I looked for a water fountain, spotted one, and walked towards it until a sign that said "Colored" warned me off. I was puzzled; I did not know why the sign was there. The realization was slow to come, but when it did, it was a pill I could not swallow —only black people could use this fountain. I was indignant; it was unfair. I was thirsty. Why were they the only ones allowed to drink from the fountain?

Baffled, I looked around and spotted a second fountain, this one boasting a sign that read, "Whites." I realized I was being told to drink from this fountain. Thirst sated, I looked back and forth between the fountains, trying to discern the difference. The fountain labeled "Whites" was newer and cleaner. The one labeled "Colored" was off-putting, marred by brown water stains and rusty piping. That was when it struck me: it was not the whites getting the short end of the deal; it was the blacks.

The wrongness of this situation was deeply grating. Why should people of color have to drink from the rusty fountain while the whites enjoy a clean one? Why should anyone be able to tell anyone else where they can drink water? The injustice of it roiled through me, building a rebellious impulse to drink out of the fountain reserved for Coloreds as if doing so would alchemically change wrong to right. As I took a step towards that shabby fountain, I considered for the first-time the clusters of teenage white boys scattered around the lobby of the theater and out on the sidewalk. All looked like James Dean wannabes: packs of cigarettes rolled up in the sleeves of their tight-fitting t-shirts as lit cigarettes drooped loosely from their mouths. They were a loud bunch, radiating sinewy strength and aggression like roosters displaying in a barnyard. That is when a glistening fear coiled within me. I knew, without knowing how that a white boy drinking out of the Colored fountain would bring dangerous attention. I imagined being yelled at or beaten up, the angry tantrums so loud in my mind that they could have been shouted, "Who the fuck are you? What the fuck are you doing?"

Within seconds, my urge to drink from the Colored fountain, to transform wrong into right, evaporated as fear overwhelmed courage, and shame grew in place of pride. Just that quickly, I was wrenched from a strong, upholder-of-the-right sense of myself to that of a craven, slinking, cowardly me. This transformation, so pitilessly wrung from within, occurred without a word spoken or anyone noticing a thing.

Troubled, that afternoon, I asked my parents about the two fountains. To my surprise, they were not discomfited by their existence, only by my questioning the *rightness* of it.

As they groped for a response, I sensed fear stemming from my mother and was even more shocked to realize her concern was for me. She was telegraphing, "Harm will come to you if you persist in questioning such things."

At this point, Dad donned his mantle as the head of the family and essentially explained there was a caste system and that "Negroes" were lesser than whites. That they were lazy and untrustworthy and not only needed but wanted someone to tell them what to do. With this pronouncement, my parents rested their case, having satisfied their unease, without resolving mine. Over the ensuing months, whenever I went to the movies, I glanced at the fountains and chided myself for continuing to be bothered by the situation. I would tell myself, *Accept that they just are; they always have been and always will be. It's just the way it is. By what arrogance do I, a child, dare question their rightness? What is wrong with me that I cannot accept what everyone else, older, far more experienced, and wiser than me, considers self-evident?*

Several months later, I made a far-reaching discovery. While bending down for a sip of water from the "Whites" fountain, I sensed something different. I looked around, but the two fountains were still there, and the "coloreds" still sat on the balcony. As I brooded on this, I had an epiphany: what had changed was not something outside of me but something within. I was having a visceral reaction, not only to the Colored water fountain as dirty and repellent but now to the blacks themselves. Where once their bigger lips and broader noses had merely appeared different, they now leaned toward repulsive.

With this realization, I felt diminished, changed materially in a way that had been outside my awareness and choosing. Then, I understood: *Oh! This is how you catch racism. It creeps up on you through hidden threats and explicit statements*, subtly training your mind and body.

Later in life, I would learn that the child's boundaries between self and others are not well-formed, leaving the child susceptible to implicit and explicit messages from the world around him. This way, prejudice arises from sensing and feeling, not reason. What passes for thinking follows unhurriedly behind, solely in service of self-justification.

At age nine, the ever-present peer and cultural pressure to fit in, combined with my parents' endorsement, was eroding my allegiance to the disquieting weight of the wrongness of the situation. The acquisition of racist feelings was transforming me from the isolation and disquiet of my solitary position in southern society toward the rewards of belonging to the group. My only question, *Why don't I feel good about it?*

Looking back, I may not have recognized or doubted the rightness of this situation had I always lived in that Southern town, exposed to segregation and prejudice with no perspective rendering countervailing experiences. Perhaps, it was only the fact that I had moved five times in my first eight years and been exposed to different cultures and social norms that provided me with the contrast necessary to recognize the evil afoot in Montgomery, Alabama.

Now I better understand the anger and fear emanating from the black people of that shantytown some sixty years ago. Aside from whatever I represented to them, what would have happened if some accident had befallen me through no fault of their own? Would they be subjected to an unreasoning "punish first and ask questions later" reaction from the white community? Why not? That is the way my dad functioned.

The other thing I noticed during my visit to that shantytown was that no one acknowledged my presence. What had not registered at the time was that this had subliminally conveyed to me a sense of power and superiority: although resenting my presence, none of those people dared challenge me. Why would this be? I could well imagine white adults confronting me if I were someplace they felt I did not belong. But now, I understand, or at least think I do. They did not dare risk challenging somebody from the white community any more than I would dare to question my dad or the existence of two water fountains in the movie theater. In such ways, the violence of racism does damage even when hidden from view.

I share this memory to describe a dynamic in all family and societal life. That our assumptions and prejudices develop in the supposedly protective confines of our families regardless of social prominence or level of education, often unnoticed and unquestioned, as *just the way things are,* contributing to the unseen waters of one's life. Thus, it is not uncommon for a patient to describe a "perfectly happy childhood," never thinking to mention that neither parent ever held him nor told him he was loved.

Similarly, despite all evidence to the contrary, I felt I had grown up in a "normal family," even an exemplary one, until I began examining my family relationships in psychotherapy. There, I moved from an initial reaction of insult that my therapist would question my parents' behaviors to seeing the previously unseen waters of my life while feeling irrationally disloyal for presuming to do so. I came to appreciate that normal does not always mean healthy and certainly does not mean right.

Of course, there will always be people aware of something wrong. But such considerations erode under the relentless cultural chorus as the unexamined beliefs become increasingly normal, even if the feeling of normalcy never fully arrives. They begin to feel a part of us, making them all the harder to notice, much less question or change.

The crucial thing to realize is that questioning and thinking are foundational to the privilege of living our lives. However, it takes fortitude to have one's own mind, to stand outside the crowd, and to question the governing norm. Of course, none of this is easily done in childhood, a time of extraordinary vulnerability and marginality. The role of a child, romanticized in fantasy yet demonstrated as one of weakness and ignorance in many interactions with the adult world, induces the child to defensively internalize the situation so that it becomes like a part of himself, a second, or first, nature.

Thus, from the unseen waters of our lives, the shells of the Russian Nesting Doll accumulate, co-opting what we perceive, how we relate, and who we can imagine ourselves to be.

CHAPTER 4

Uprooted

By age eight, I had lived in: Tennessee, Oklahoma, California, and two towns in Alabama, just the places I recall. Here, I am merely reciting facts and not their implications. Facts that don't convey the disruption and upheaval created in the fabric of my existence: the rending of relationships, leaving one school and entering another, leaving behind one home to slowly turn a strange house into another home before leaving it as well. There is also an impact on extended family relationships: grandparents, aunts, uncles, and cousins. These people, the roots of my origins, I barely knew. And there was no such thing as a hometown: I was not from any place, nor was there any place to which I would return—life was a wandering, rootless journey with no destination in mind.

It was in this context that, aside from the continued threat of emotional and physical violence in my family, to which I was accustomed, and of the potential for racial violence around me, I felt comparatively secure and happy in Montgomery, Alabama. There was a growing sense of routine and order in my world: a rhythm that lent structure, stability, and predictability.

For the first time, I had a best buddy, Greg Cook, and a sense of belonging. The wonder of that time is captured in my memory of Greg and me flitting like shadows through the Alabama woods and coming upon a dilapidated shack. On the rickety porch sat an old, wizened black woman. Her head crowned with steel-wool hair, and her face boasted a mouth of tattered yellow teeth framed by spittle-laden lips. Dark eyes gleaming in the dim light, she called out, "Dayawantyafortunered." Neither Greg nor I had any idea what she was saying, but not wanting to be rude, I kept trying to clarify, "What?"

She repeated, "Dayawantyafortunered."

After several concentrated attempts, I managed to decipher the stream of syllables, "Do you want your fortune read?" At that instant, electricity coursed through my body: magic was at hand.

Greg and I approached cautiously, ready to flee if anything untoward stirred the air. The woman asked for a coin, and I fished a nickel out of my pocket. Using a cane, she heaved her stick-figured, bowed body out of her squeaky rocking chair and scuttled through the open door, tattered dress loosely swinging from her bony shoulders and flapping around her scrawny legs.

The impenetrable gloom of the inner recesses of her shack signaled caution while promising countless mysteries. Warily, my eyes struggling to acclimate to the dim interior, I followed her in. As my eyes adjusted, I noticed that inside this shadow-world stood a worn wooden table in a single room, upon which lay a thick, tattered paperback book, a large needle, almost the size of a knitting needle but much sharper, rested on it. The Witch waited for us to gather around, then, with astonishing speed, grabbed the needle and drove it forcefully into the book. Startled, we jumped back, on the brink of flight, as The Witch cackled in delight. She then opened the tome to the page the needle pointed.

"Diswilltellyafutah."

We listened intently, drawing close, trying to catch every syllable.

"Ya will..."

But it was no use. As the witch prattled on, Greg and I looked at each other with confusion, our faces contorted with concentration. Neither of us could understand a word of what she was saying.

Regrettably, our fortune was to remain a mystery. Still, we stayed, soaking up the Witch's voice, our bodies supercharged with that magical moment as fantasy and reality coalesced.

Those summer days in Montgomery were some of the happiest of my life. I was waking to myself. My adventures with Greg and the hours spent playing red light, green light with all the children in the neighborhood until dusk turned to night, of walking to the A & W Root Beer stand in the asphalt bubbling heat of the day, the frosty mug of root beer sure to give me a headache, remain some of the happiest moments in my life. For the first time, I belonged. Lost in the thrill of adventure and play, watching as days slipped by contentedly, I could forget the familiar ugliness of reality.

Then, one night at dinner, we were all sitting around the table when I felt tension in the air. I looked around to understand its source, but everything was normal. Mutti, an apron around her waist, was placing plates of food on the table, and all the boys were yakking away while preparing to dive in and eat fast to be first to get to the limited seconds. Yet, something was off; I could feel it. Once my mother took her seat, it did not take long for all to become clear. My dad announced, “We’ll be leaving Montgomery soon. We’re moving to a place called Hanau, Germany.”

The air went out of me, and the smile left my face. My throat began closing, my chest constricting; it wasn’t fair. Just as I was getting used to being happy and secure, everything would be taken away: school, Greg, Montgomery, all gone. Everything I had come to hold dear snuffed out like a candle upon a blizzard. My life, like a beach, was about to be swept clean of footprints by the tide.

What was even the point of holding on to things when they only get taken away? The lesson I learned that night? That life, like the tide, brings things in and takes things away, and nothing is guaranteed except the tide, and the tide is unrelenting.

CHAPTER 5

A Galaxy Far Away

After seventeen hours on a propeller-driven plane, starved of sleep and vomiting during the landing, I arrived in Hanau, Germany. Collapsing onto the hotel bed without undressing, I'm awoken, seemingly seconds later, by Dad commanding, "Get up. It's time to eat." Fortunately, hunger soon supplants the nausea of fatigue as the tantalizing smells of stuffed cabbage and quartered potatoes waft through the air.

Situated on the T of the forested road that pointed like an arrow to the Army Fort where Dad was a battalion commander, the hotel provided a front-row seat from our second-story window to the early morning maneuvers. These entailed deploying tanks and 8" howitzers, weighing 60,000 pounds each, to the border with communist Germany, in the never-ending practice of war.

The thrumming power and intensity of the entire event remain with me to this day. The predawn maneuvers always began with a forewarning, a sound like the sonorous growl of lions on the prowl, which grew ever louder and more menacing as the behemoths neared yet remained veiled by the morning fog. As the floor begins to tremble beneath my feet, the machines of war emerge like wraiths, one by one, eerily materializing and dematerializing in the mist that swirled around them. At last, fully revealed, the tanks and cannon stand as grand as tall ships sailing across a leaden sea.

Nine weeks later, we moved to a two-story stone and slate-roofed house attached to a burnt-out factory. A narrow river was situated just yards away, having run a paddle wheel for the factory in decades past. In winter, the river froze over, its crystalline surface beckoning my brothers and me to skate, our ankles buckling under the weight of our bodies. In the spring, flooded by melting snows, the river electrified the air as it roared its approval to the change in seasons.

Under gray skies, with an occasionally glorious sunny day thrown in, my brothers and I spun our fantasies into life within the factory walls, running through the sodden light of cavernous rooms as gargoyle stubs of burnt beams peered down from above.

The custodian, an unkempt man dressed in stained overalls, and boasting a scruffy gray beard, kept a cow and a pig. Each morning, he milked the cow into a metal bucket, creating a grating, pissing-like sound that only added to the pungent odor of straw and dung, which hung thick in the air.

One morning, I entered the cobblestone courtyard and spied the custodian with another man in the doorway of the shed, the pig at his feet. There was a sharp pop, and the pig collapsed like a marionette whose strings had been cut. After several throbbing heartbeats, I realized the custodian had shot the pig in the head. In horrid fascination, I watched as the two men grasped a rusty chain from a pulley above their heads, wrapped it around the pig's hind legs, and, grunting with effort, pulled it jerkily into the air. There, the custodian stilled the pig's swaying motion with one hand while deftly cutting it from pelvis to chest with a knife in the other, intestines spilling like boiled spaghetti into a steaming pile on the frosted cobblestones. In such ways, I discovered that life and death were forever intertwined, always dancing hand in hand.

Much was good at this time in my life, replete with raw experiences and new adventures and discoveries, but unknown to me, that was not the case for my dad. The soldiers, tightly strung from the incessant maneuvers, broke out in a riot at a bar. The commander of the fort arrived to restore order. While inside, soldiers escaped from the rear and turned his car over with his wife inside. Shortly after, my father assumed command of the fort.

Years later, I learned that Dad suffered several "nervous breakdowns" during this time. Given his frequent absence, his hospitalizations went unnoticed by the kids. After years of treating narcissists, I could well imagine the cause of his breakdown. He lacked the psychological infrastructure necessary for coping with less than heroic results. To his shame, he discovered he was not the mythical hero showcased in his stories. In the harsh light of a brutal reality, Jim Bowie and Davey Crockett were nowhere to be found.

Dad was transferred to Heidelberg, Germany. In the past, it was customary for the family to follow behind. This time, however, I was to accompany him. I was not happy about leaving my family behind and being forced into sole proximity to Dad, but I had no say. For the next six months, I lived with him in a single room in the BOQ (Bachelor Officers' Quarters), sleeping on a cot and eating at the officers' club. On warm days, I washed the cars of the other officers for pocket money and played by myself. The main negative was Dad. Always conscious of appearance, he was continually barking at me to "straighten up, head up, back straight!" On the positive side, there was a kind of intimacy in sharing dinner and evening snacks, knee to knee, in the small confines of his single room. I grew to love smoked oysters out of a tin and crackers with cheese.

When fall came, my family had still not arrived, but that did not stop the surprises from coming. Instead of attending the American elementary school within walking distance, I would make the daily bus trip to the school for children of the French military in Spire, Germany. There, forbidden to speak English and initiated into the confusion and fear of not understanding what the teachers were saying, I had difficulty sorting out how to please them. I lived in dread. Rulers striking tender hands, reddened ears pulled, and saliva spewed by teachers yelling like drill instructors became the rule of the day. In this shock-and-awe fashion, I learned the vital importance of being able to make sense of things and the danger that arises when one does not.

Eventually, housing became available, and the rest of the family arrived. As we were beginning to get back to a semblance of normalcy and stability, my parents made yet another announcement: Jacques, Edward, and I were going to a boarding school in France.

Again, I was left breathless. I had just been reunited with my family, seemingly only moments ago, and now I was to lose them again. I couldn't fathom it. Was this the way life was supposed to be? I protested; we all did. Mutti exclaimed, "It will be a Great Adventure and a fantastic opportunity for you to expand your cultural horizons," with a brilliant smile that defied acknowledgment of the angst Jacques, Edward, and I were exhibiting.

We begged, "Please, Mom, don't make us go. I don't want to go!" "No. No. No!" we cried in unison, our panic plain for anyone to see.

Mutti, overcome by the intensity of our distress, looked at us, mouth open and eyebrows drawn. Finally, at wit's end, she ordered, "Go talk to your father."

In front of Dad, we dropped to our knees and begged to be allowed to stay home. "Please, we don't want to go, don't make us go," Edward said between sniffles. Even Jacques, who always went along with whatever the parents wanted, echoed Ed's cries. Though fully involved in the appeals to be allowed to stay home, another part of my mind felt the cold growing certainty that our fate was already sealed.

I watched Dad's face contort, nose scrunched, and upper lip drawn back, all harbingers of what his response would be. In a tone laden with disgust, he responded, "Stop c-c-crying like b-b-b-b-babies. I'll hear no more a-a-a-about this. You're going, and that's it."

Some things you cannot change; some things must only be endured. What I did not fully appreciate, what I could not have possibly foreseen, was not only that the tide was going out, but it was going way, way out, forewarning the mind-boggling destruction of a coming tsunami.

The Etienne Boys: Jacques, Charles, Edward

CHAPTER 6

The Abyss: Free Fall

Our Great Adventure began on a frigid, bright, sunny day, seeming as though the world was mocking me, gloating over my misery.

Always, the station wagon had been an extension of my home, taking us safely throughout Europe. But today, it hummed along, impervious to my despair as I sat stiff with apprehension, slotted alongside my brothers in the backseat.

The car was only following my parents' lead; its indifferent attitude mirrored theirs as they chattered mindlessly in the front seat, refusing to acknowledge our misery. I felt utterly alone. Worn down mentally and emotionally, I sought refuge in my only warmth: the blanket of my despair.

After traveling many miles, a burgeoning sense of urgency emanating from the front seat pulled me from my dark cocoon. I soon understood that Dad felt a recurring jolt through the steering wheel and was concerned about car trouble. As apprehension crossed my mother's face, hope flared in mine. Wishfully, I thought, *The car hadn't betrayed me; it had only been biding its time.* As I waited to see what would unfold, I became aware for the first time that I was rhythmically thumping my head against the back seat. Suddenly, I understood. I was the source of the jolting that so unsettled my father. Fearing his anger, I willed myself to be still; it was not easy.

The car powered onward, carrying us along two-lane roads that wound through postcard German towns and villages, across stone bridges spanning turbulent streams, and alongside dung-scented fields upon which farmers labored in the distance. On we went, ever farther from home, toward a town that, to me, despite its inherent beauty, would always be as cold and gray as burnt coal—Strasbourg, France.

As Dad parked the car on the cobblestone street, I had my first glimpse of Collège St. Etienne. It was three stories of a slate-roofed stone building in the shape of an H; one end was closed off by a fifteen-foot-high wall capped with incisors of jagged green and brown glass fragments. As we approached the gaping maw of the entrance, I wondered: *Are the walls to keep people in or to keep people out?*

Inside the belly of the courtyard stood an old stone church under reconstruction, surrounded by mounds of dirt from which bones protruded like the spikes of a sea urchin: the remains of an ancient cemetery uprooted by the digging. Adding to this phantasmagoric scene was the jabber of French parents and children excitedly bidding their farewells, a festive mood in jarring contrast to my own. Panic-stricken, I turned to my parents, another appeal to stop this madness scrabbling up my throat, only to encounter the actors playing their roles.

Recognizing the futility, resignation set in, as did my self-questioning: *What's wrong with me? My brothers don't seem to feel this way, though they are unusually quiet. Am I the only one? Why can't I, too, see it as a Great Adventure? My parents wouldn't leave us in a dangerous place, would they? Why don't I trust them?*

This self-questioning only subsided when the long-dreaded moment arrived and passed with stunning indifference. My mother hugged me. I held tight, burying my face in the scratchy wool of her stylish gray coat. Then, she pulled away, cold air slapping my cheeks where warmth had just been. With dead eyes, I watched as Mutti turned away and followed my father out of that courtyard and out of my life. I stood in heart-dropping shock.

After a few moments, I began wondering what we were supposed to do when a movement caught my eye. A priest, about forty and of average build, with pale corpse skin, ice-blue eyes above cold-reddened cheeks, and dark hair pomaded back from a high forehead, was striding determinedly toward us, his black cape fluttering behind. This vampiric figure began roughly pushing my brothers and me in different directions and into distinct lines of students that, I would soon discover, went to separate places. That quickly, I was shorn of my entire family, isolated in a sea of strangeness. Adrift, I felt an aloneness that was far more alone than I knew alone could be.

Dazed, I mindlessly followed the line into a large hall filled with worn wooden tables set with plates and utensils. Mimicking the other kids, I stood behind my chair with no idea of what I was waiting for when there was a sharp tap on my shoulder. Turning my head, I looked up into the unwelcoming eyes of a young man. He spoke, the sounds a garble to me. His tone was as frigid as his appearance. Wishfully wanting safe refuge, I willed myself to imagine he was asking if I was okay. I smiled tentatively and said, "Wee."

That is when he kicked my legs from under me. As I fell to the floor, he began thumping me with his feet, herding me, like an animal, in a circle until I finally arrived back at the chair. Traumatized, heart thundering in my chest, I desperately struggled to comply as he motioned for me to stand. Dizzy, rising on unsteady legs, and fearful of falling, I clung to the back of the chair for support. To my alarm, he only became more infuriated. Angrily, he repeatedly jabbed his finger at my arms. Terrified, drowning in a rip tide of uncertainty, I looked around, desperate to sort out what he wanted.

That was when I noticed the other children all had their arms crossed. Dread-filled, fearful of falling, yet fearing worse if I did not, I gave up my grip on the chair and quickly crossed my arms, praying that this was the desired response. Begrudgingly, the surveillant stood looking at me without saying a thing, his silence only fueling my anxiety, then begrudgingly moved on down the line.

Standing there, deprived of my steadying hold on the chair, I began to wobble. Then, in a desperate attempt to retain my balance, my eyes fell upon the badly scratched back of the chair, discovering that its scored surface provided a steadying point of focus and balance. That was when I made an important discovery: in the dimmest of hours, something as small and meaningless as the scratched back of a chair can become the most precious thing in the world. As insignificant and lifeless as it was, the back of that chair provided something known and stable and became a world where I could take refuge from the one that had gone completely mad beyond its borders. Thus, I escaped into its labyrinthian weave and the safer place it promised.

Minutes later, The Priest, leading a procession of faculty, self-importantly ambles into the hall and onto the dais that held the faculty dining table. After a short prayer, the faculty took their seats, and we were finally permitted to take ours. On cue, kitchen staff flooded the room, placing large metal bowls on the tables. The one nearest me was filled with pieces of meat, each boasting the severed end of a white artery sticking out like a rubber tube. I had never seen such meat before and scurried to name it, stumbling upon the likeliest answer given its shape: tongue. Another bowl contained white mush drowning beneath a cloudy pool of water; I guessed mashed potatoes. I did not eat that night except for a piece of bread and two squares of chocolate that passed for dessert.

Following dinner, The Priest, his black cape once again billowing behind, shepherded us up shadowed marble stairs and along high-ceilinged hallways sharply echoing with the footsteps of our passage. We arrived at a large rectangular room with an uneven wood-planked floor holding three rows of beds, maybe thirty in all. One long wall had windows overlooking a canal with a fountain. A shorter wall nearest the entrance featured a metal trough running its length; a row of faucets like the beaks of blackbirds poked their heads out from above. The short wall at the opposite end of the rectangle contained a cubicle for the surveillants—those creatures charged with keeping us in line, one of whom had introduced me to this new world with kicks.

I was assigned a bed next to a window overlooking the fountain, insanely grateful for the view but more so for the tiniest illusion of privacy afforded by not being hemmed in on all sides by strangers. Standing by the window in the months to come, I would discover that the fountain had a life of its own as its waters danced to the tunes of the changing seasons and stopped dancing altogether in Winter's icy embrace.

A giant pillow serving as a duvet covered the bed. At its foot sat a locker, a washrag perched on top, and my meager belongings on the floor next to it. Having learned to take my cue from the others, I stored my things and, braving the cold, stripped to my underwear. Shivering, washrag in hand, I waited in line for my turn at the trough: my first French bath. I soon discovered that each faucet had one handle—no hot water. In the winter months to come, the taps froze, icicles hanging like fangs of saber-tooth tigers from their gullets; except for weekly trips to an indoor swimming pool, bathing was inconceivable. Later, when we visited home, our stench was a marvel to our parents, as was the quarter-inch thick coat of grime on the sides of the tub when we bathed.

Laying in bed at the end of that first day, surrounded by darkness and thirty foreigners whom I could not understand, my despair caught up with me. I struggled to muffle my sobs, my grief warring with my fear of dangerous attention. Hurtling into this first night away from home, I caught myself thumping my head against the pillow. My last thought before sleep captured me: *Please let this be a nightmare from which I will soon awake.*

Morning came in a cacophony of light and sound as ceiling lights blazed on, and the faucets angrily spewed water into the metal trough with a reverberating roar. The surveillants ran up and down the aisles, maniacally shouting, "Allez vous! Allez vous!" adding to the sensory assault and feeling of alarm.

My clamoring heart quieted as I realized this was no life-threatening emergency but only the surveillants taking sadistic delight in rocketing us without care into the pre-dawn of a new day. The first full day of my Great Adventure had begun.

No question, I was a victim of Collège St. Etienne and felt victimized by my parents for leaving me there, but I could not afford to know it at the time. I assumed there must be some reason for this exile into a strange world and that if I had difficulty coping, that was on me. My feelings, largely unidentified, scampered like feral children, their dark eyes darting wildly. If I had known their names, they would have included never-ending fear, spirit-sapping helplessness, and eviscerating loneliness. Regardless, I had one family rule to hang on to—never give up. I fought back.

On the first day of class, I wore earbuds to listen to my transistor radio even though knowing this could not possibly be allowed. The teacher discovered it and confiscated the radio. On another occasion, in the middle of the night, an accomplice and I crept out of the dorm and snuck into the church. In the light of the moon streaming through the windows, I discovered a hole behind the altar filled with bones. Selecting a large one, I threw it out the narrow archers' window into the public street beyond; yells of shocked surprise echoed in return. My accomplice and I laughed, enjoying our journey into the spare joys of sadistic delight.

My signature moment of revolutionary zeal occurred when I brought back a large bag of marbles after a visit home. I had noticed that the dorm floor canted toward the cubicle in which the surveillants slept. An hour after lights out, I slipped from my bed and crept to the top of the room near the trough. There, I eased the marbles onto the floor and, with gentle pushes, sent them on their way before swiftly returning to bed. The marbles click-clacked over the ancient floorboards toward the doorway to the surveillants' cubicle. My anticipation grew: could this work? Soon, I had my answer. A surveillant came out to investigate the noise and stepped upon the marbles in his bare feet. Repeatedly cursing and yipping in pain and surprise, he hopped from one foot to another. Furious, the surveillants rousted the students, made us strip our beds, and empty our lockers. It was in vain; they found nothing, and there were no witnesses.

Even so, I had earned a reputation and was convicted of the crime. The surveillants forced me outside, where I had to stand barefoot, in my pajamas, in the dark and cold of the cobblestone courtyard. I imagine they thought this punishment would chasten me, but my spirit soared on the ivory chimes of my chattering teeth. I felt free and alive, no longer an insignificant cog in someone else's universe. I was learning how action could supplant depression, at least temporarily.

The perversities continued. When I contracted *la grippe* (the flu), the staff, noting my high fever, housed me in the infirmary with its working radiator. Late that night, The Priest entered, bathed in the devilish glow cast by a red-light bulb above the door. As I watched him approach through fevered eyes, he exuded false joviality. He sat on the edge of the bed, leaned forward, and whispered into my ear, "Oh, La Grande American, you're not so grand now, are you?"

Given that I had never felt like the Great American, I realized I was merely a stand-in for despised Americans. I felt a twang of pride, knowing that for this fool to take the time to visit an eleven-year-old in a sick ward in the middle of the night to perform such a petty act of malice was proof positive that this Grande American had gotten under his lizard skin.

I do not want to portray everything as bad at Collège St. Etienne, just most things. I discovered some of the marvels of France: intensely flavored ice creams and pastries, beautiful city parks, the smell of roasting chestnuts drifting from kiosks along wintry city streets, streetlamps twinkling on snowy nights, grand buildings, and *steak au poivre,* to name a few. I also began smoking Gauloises cigarettes. But, these were fleeting pleasures in the scale of things, soon snuffed out by the ongoing vacuum of care. It was in these dismal circumstances that I had a revelation: one can grow to hate something precisely because it is loved. In this instance, I am thinking of my parents' visits, which occurred every four to six weeks. On warm days, they would take us out for a picnic. My mother would spread a blanket and serve her oven-roasted chicken and homemade potato salad, a ritual that only reignited memories of home. I loved the food, I loved my mom, and I hated those visits. They became a cruel tease, inciting memory and desire, reminding me of all I had lost and would soon lose again. At first, my grief reignited upon my parents' every departure, but, over time, knowing what was to come, it flared up upon their every arrival. I came to hate these visits knowing the heartbreak they promised.

After fifteen months at Collège St. Etienne, I was suffering stomach pain so acute it bent me over and dropped me to the floor. At first, on a visit home, the Army doctors recommended powdered milk, given the absence of homogenized milk at Ecole St. Etienne. Unsurprisingly, it did not help. Curiously though, back at Ecole St. Etienne, I did find the nightly ritual of preparing and drinking the foul-tasting brew oddly comforting. Something so small and inconsequential became important because it provided a personal routine, a mooring, and perhaps most notably, something all my own in a world in which little was mine. This nightly practice buttressed my embattled spirit in the frigid winds of this abysmal existence. The fact that I grew to like the taste tells all.

Finally, three months later, my body had achieved what words and tears had been unable to accomplish. Fearing the development of an ulcer, the doctors recommended I return home. Several months later, my brothers followed when Mutti, during a visit, found Jacques's mattress lying in a cavernous hallway—his punishment for some infraction. This debasing act, directly witnessed by my mother, breached the walls of her denial. Furious, she confronted The Priest and, with my brothers in tow, quit the school forever.

You might ask why my parents kept us in this place; I certainly did. My mother's protestations that it was to expand our cultural horizons were far from compelling. In later years, I did not care that my siblings and their spouses groaned whenever I raised the subject. They wanted to sweep the past away without understanding it—for me, this was impossible; I had to make sense of things to have any hope of trusting again.

I never got a convincing answer from my parents. However, I did not fail. Over the years, I pieced together a story from circumstantial evidence that put reason to our ordeal.

Years later, when touring Canada with Mutti, Michelle discovered that she had attended Catholic boarding schools from age four. I had not known that mom was separated from her family at such an early age. I could readily imagine four-year-old Mutti in those bastions of structure, stricture, and faith, receiving validation and approval for her other-oriented, selfless behavior and steadfast devotion. Her nightly ritual of kneeling at her bedside, dressed in a cotton nightgown, head bent, eyes closed, and hands prayerfully clasped in front of her, had always reminded me of a little girl. And now, I knew why. I could see the thread of that ritual weaving its way back to her childhood and forward to the day of her death. She had discovered her own routines that held her throughout her life, where her parents' arms would not. Given a depressed, repeatedly psychiatrically hospitalized mother, the death of her brother, and an alcoholic father, I could well imagine that for my mom, boarding school might have provided reason and structure that served as a positive alternative to her sad and debilitating home life. Still, I could not fathom the devastating loss any four-year-old would feel in being separated from home, any home.

Another piece of the puzzle was something about my mother that I knew from personal experience: she was loving and caring but could be a lioness when it came to protecting her family. She was strong that way, doing what had to be done, at least as she saw it. I could well envision her whisking us off to Catholic boarding school so our father had a quiet place to recover, free from the noise and energies of her three oldest boys.

I only wish she had told me if this was the case. Then, I could have imbued my losses with meaning and purpose. Looking out for the family is a value to which I intensely subscribe. It was precisely that value that appeared breached when Jacques, Ed, and I were exiled to that Kafkaesque existence without a convincing explanation or a sympathetic ear. At the same time, I recognize that Dad's narcissistic vulnerability would have been triggered by anything that gave the lie to his omnipotent presentation of himself. How ironic that my mother's attempt to look out for the family might have been the cause of our not being looked out for at all.

CHAPTER 7

The World Is Changed

War is said to be an experience of days, weeks, or months of boredom shattered by seconds of violence. That description loosely fits my life. People were not shooting at me, but I was repeatedly turned inside out and upside down with little warning. The abiding apprehension of the inevitable slap, a sudden change in living situation, a kick in the back, or exile to a foreign land did the trick. Anticipatory dread was an enduring element of my existence.

But now, at twelve, I was older and hardened, no longer grief-stricken or surprised by adverse events. Where previously I had felt there had been an "us" of the family, I knew there was just "*me*" and the world with which *I* had to contend. I braced for the worst; in fact, I expected it. I had been in the abyss and escaped uninjured, or so I thought. I did not appreciate that, on the inside, I had turned into a dark, brooding soul in an antagonistic relationship to the world. And this was repeatedly proven to be justified as my father threw another surprise at me.

Home represented civilization, and civilization was in Patrick Henry Village, Heidelberg, Germany. My father, for reasons known only to himself, lobbied the school system to admit me to the ninth grade rather than the seventh, where I belonged at age twelve. He argued that French education was superior and to place me in the seventh grade would hold me back. His will prevailed because it was a school for military dependents, and he was an officer. Yet again, I entered a foreign environment, this one called high school, in the middle of the academic year. Not surprisingly, I floundered right away, but that was nothing new. Floundering had become a way of life.

I joined the high school soccer team because of my love for the game, learned in the courtyard of Collège St. Etienne, and instantly became its smallest and slowest member. I remember playing a German team comprised of six-footers, begging the coach to put me in. He reluctantly granted my wish with several minutes remaining in a blow-out loss. I ran onto the field, dreaming of saving the day, only then appreciating that I was a dwarf among giants. But that did not deter me: I gritted my teeth and ran harder. Unfortunately, my mind had written feats of greatness that my body could not cash. The harder I ran, the more my limbs flailed in all directions, slowing me to a crawl. People were laughing, including members of the German team, who, smirking, looked down at me. But that was not the humiliation it once would have been; scorn was an old acquaintance. And had I been on the sidelines, I probably would have laughed too.

Ironically, my biggest nemesis academically was English: I was failing. I had lost three years of schooling in English grammar between Spire Academy and Collège St. Etienne and then missed the fourth and fifth years when I hopscotched into the ninth grade. After struggling to learn French, I spoke and dreamt in it fluently. English, however, could have as well be rocket science. Understanding the parts of speech and English grammar eluded me. To me, the term "dangling participle" sounded uncomfortably close to male genitalia. But I did not care; I was used to failure and pretty good at it.

What I did care about, though, was my father's wrath. Accordingly, I set out to steal the English 9th-grade final exam. Unfortunately, as things usually go, another student happened upon me and sulkily insisted on inclusion. Several days later, I was summoned to the principal's office and confronted with my crime. Like any good soldier or thief, for that matter, I stoically denied it all. So, it was a surreal moment when after all the denials, a small voice squeaked from behind: "I've told him everything." It was the other student. Bastard! Whatever happened to the military edict to give only name, rank, and serial number, not to mention the notion of honor among thieves and not being a rat? Dad did the predictable.

All was not bad in Heidelberg, just nearly so; I had no friends. The kids in high school were older and bigger, and the kids my age went to a different school. I spent my time alone, sometimes visiting the swimming pool during summer, where I pretended not to envy the camaraderie of the kids around me.

Lounging upon the grass, basking in the warmth of the sun, I looked up at the diving platform that pierced the blue sky. Kids clambered up the rungs, rushed to the edge, then flung themselves off, screaming with delight. I thought, *I can do that,* and soon was making my way up the ladder. It was then I noticed that what did not look high while lying securely on the ground below became more Mount Everest-like with each rung ascended. Thirty-nine rungs and thirty feet later, white-knuckling the ladder, I was seriously wondering what had possessed me.

Surrounded by open air, besieged by vertigo, and panting anxiously, I crawled ignominiously onto the concrete platform, keeping the guard rail in a tight grip. There, I screwed up enough courage to pull myself into a crouch and then, grudgingly, hand over hand along the rail. In this manner, I tottered to the lip of the platform.

Here, I made another discovery; the pool was a blur without my glasses. I could see its outline but not the clear water within. *How was I to prepare myself for entry if I could not see it coming?* As I stood there, wrestling with fear, seconds morphed into minutes, and minutes into more minutes. My embarrassment grew as kid after kid worked their way by me, some throwing questioning looks before shrugging and joyously leaping into the void.

Sick to my stomach with fear, I considered exiting the way I had come—back down the ladder. But that way was cut off as I imagined my cowardly descent on full display for all to see. So, again, I pulled myself to the edge of the platform. There my imagination would not let go of me. I envisioned jumping only to cartwheel out of control and land face-first on the surface of the water below.

Thus, like a metronome, I tick-tocked between the ladder and the edge, between shame on one side and terror on the other. Finally, so wretched I could stand no more, I moved to the front of the platform, took a deep breath, and leaped; *my* scream held no glee. I hit the water, the flats of my feet stinging and plunged to the bottom of the pool as clouds of bubbles billowed past me. Soon I followed, thinking: *That wasn't so bad!*

Angrily, I climbed that platform repeatedly, consciously pulverizing the fear that minutes earlier had been crushing me. I learned four things that day: one, things look different depending on where you stand; two, fantasy is more frightening than reality; three, you can conquer your fear by doing what you fear; and four, point your toes when plunging into water from a height.

Combating my abiding sense of isolation was an ongoing challenge. I had not yet turned the magic thirteen, the "teen" part of the word holding all the magic. That did not matter; I began sneaking into the Teen Club through the back door. There, I discovered I had a natural eye for shooting pool and, after several months, could make difficult shots, albeit not consistently. Nonetheless, on better days, I would string together a series of shots that showed the older players in a bad light.

There was only one pool table, and all the testosterone-filled boys lined the walls, impatiently waiting their turn while trash-talking one another. The winner of each game held the table while the loser walked the gauntlet of shame back to the end of the line. The problem was that losing to me was particularly galling to some of my older and bigger opponents.

One such brute was named Jesse, who was a member of the high school wrestling team. During his walk back to the end of the line, his buddies taunted him, "Hey Jesse, that little guy smoked your ass, didn't he? Maybe you should ask him for lessons." I was chalking my cue stick, feeling full of myself, and preparing for my next opponent when a pool stick whipped across my throat from behind, choking me. It was Jesse, taking his embarrassment out on me. Painfully, I pushed against the cue, angrily hissing, "Get off me, you half-breed," thus providing the excuse he needed to challenge me to a fight.

I knew I had no chance of winning, but refusing a fight frightened me more than losing one. So, we went outside, and Jesse proceeded to beat me without mercy. However, he's the one who quit. I made him afraid. Not of me—I never laid a hand on him—but of the damage he was inflicting: my face distended; eyelids engorged to the size of golf balls; one eye swollen shut, the other nearly so; an ear torn; lips split, and blood streaming down my face and from my mouth. The damage to my gums was so extensive that a dentist commented on it fifty years later. Regardless, I got back up after each knockdown and kept getting back up until a look of growing worry traversed his face. At this, he waved me off and nervously scurried away. When I stumbled home, my mother screamed.

However, the event most carved into my psyche was what happened after I took myself to lunch in Heidelberg. The meal finished, I was hitchhiking home when an African American male, with a Caucasian female in the passenger seat, picked me up. An attractive couple, made more so by their warm and kind demeanors, we passed the time chatting amiably. All was good until the MPs (military police) pulled us over. Even at age 12, it soon became apparent that the two large helmeted white MPs were angry about a black man daring to be with a white woman and a white woman who would accept his attention. "What are you all doing?" To the woman, "Are you with this negro?" "What is your business here?" Faces twisted by malice and snarling like dogs looking for any excuse to attack; they were intent on giving this couple a hard time. As I watched the MP's bullying treatment of the couple from the back seat, anger boiled up in me, giving rise to fury and the courage to speak. I interjected myself into the MPs' tirade to divert them from whatever course they were on. "Excuse me! These people are giving me a ride home. My dad, General McCormack (I gave him a battlefield promotion), is waiting for me. He won't be happy if I'm late." The two MPs locked eyes with me, clearly questioning my authenticity, but their uncertainty grew as I steadily held their gaze. Finally, they gave in and resentfully backed off and drove away.

We drove on, no one mentioning the frightening encounter, but the atmosphere in the car had changed; the warm feelings and good cheer were stripped away and replaced by empty silence. Minutes later, the couple dropped me off at my apartment building. As I entered the front door, I turned to wave goodbye, only to discover that the MPs had returned, their jeep crowding the couple's car. I felt sickened by this ruthless display of power directed toward this gentle couple.

I wish I had returned to the couple's car and bore witness somehow. Instead, fearful of reprisals because generals do not live in apartment buildings, I slunk inside. And, just as in that Montgomery, Alabama movie theatre, in an instant, I suffered another humbling and gut-wrenching transformation from lionhearted to craven. I never learned what happened to that couple.

Several weeks later, another parental announcement: we were returning to the United States, someplace called Virginia. From my point of view, it did not matter, for every place was the same: they all sucked; there was no escape.

PART II

PUSH BACK—HATCHING 101

I was tired of being pushed around, of feeling like a cog in someone else's universe. I wanted to do more than exist. I was yearning for a more robust sense of self without knowing it. The best I could do was follow my impulses: they were the one thing I knew was mine.

CHAPTER 8

Adolescence: Lashing Out

In 1963, at age thirteen, my family returned to the United States via the SS United States. The five-day crossing allowed time to appreciate the immensity of the ocean, how tiny we humans are, and from the ship's bow, the wisdom of not spitting into the wind. It was a marvel of a ship, one of the largest of its day, boasting marble stairways, enormous crystal chandeliers, and uniformed servers ready to discern needs before needs arose.

Dad bought a house in Annandale, Virginia, and I entered W.T. Woodson H.S. as a repeating freshman. Its size astonished me: three thousand students, over 750 in my graduating class. A city unto itself that even boasted a planetarium.

After my ordeals in Europe, what once had seemed a relatively stable and predictable world now felt radically capricious. As my fellow students manifested optimism and an unfailing belief in an absolute reality, I knew the world as unstable and readily capable of turning upside down in the snap of a finger.

Lacking any sort of compass or confident sense of the future, I was adrift, swept along by the currents of the moment, hormones raging alongside an abiding readiness for the next problem to come along. I did not have a stable sense of who I was, what I wanted, or where I was going. Mired in a distrust of authority and an enduring rebelliousness, I assumed this was simply the way I was.

Ironically, by the end of my freshman year, I had unwittingly earned enough credits, when added to those carried over from Heidelberg, to qualify as a junior, again leapfrogging a year ahead through no exceptional achievement of my own.

I disliked school. I did not want to study and did not know how to study. I performed okay in classes that interested me and daydreamed through the rest until the final bell rang. Then, infused with the elixir of freedom, I would spring to life with new-found energy and embrace the rest of *my* day.

One class stands out: typing. It was repetitive and boring and taught me that boring makes hard ten times harder. The noxious part was the teacher. Not she as a person, although a bit stern and perfectly cast given her pinched face and bent bird-like figure.

Disquietingly, she pecked at me in ways not unlike my father's: "Straighten your back. Don't look at the keyboard. Touch the board lightly. No, that's wrong." Nonetheless, I could forgive her for all that. What was insufferable was her gag-worthy halitosis combined with her unfortunate tendency to lean down and speak into my ear when making corrections, thus enveloping me in the nauseating pool of her rancid breath.

Under this aversive conditioning, I began cutting class. First one, then another, and another, totaling twenty-one days in a row without that ever having been the plan. It was wishful thinking in all its glory; *Because I got away with it one day; couldn't I get away with it the next, and then the next, and so on?* A tiny voice whispered warnings that went unheeded. None of this became real to me until an acquaintance, a volunteer in the principal's office, alerted me that I would be called in and suspended.

Ever fearful of Dad's wrath, I sought a way out. Necessity fuels creativity. I would strike pre-emptively. I would turn myself in and claim an unbearably guilty conscience demanding I confess. I hoped such purity of soul and flagrant self-flogging would help mitigate my punishment. I hurried to the principal's office and straightaway asked to speak with him. Hat figuratively in hand, head bent, eyes studying the toes of my shoes, tremulous voice infused with the veracity of the angst I was feeling, I put on a world-class performance of Catholic guilt incarnate.

The principal, moved by my presentation, compassionately decided not to suspend me but advised me that he still had to tell my parents. Flooded with worry, I girded myself for another interminable lecture and the staccato drumbeat of my father's stuttering, punctuated by slaps to the face. I also worried about Mom; she would be upset, and I hated disappointing her. My despair must have been writ large, for unsolicited, the principal rushed to assure me that he would speak to them on my behalf—hope found, lost, and found again.

On this rare occasion, it seemed my parents had spoken about how to handle the situation: Their response was thoughtful rather than reactive. In truth, Dad had no response at all. Unusually, Mom did all the talking. Briefly, she scolded me for skipping class, then with astonishing alacrity and ill-disguised pride, jumped to praising me for having done "the right thing" in confessing. She was basking in the vice principal's vouching for me. With his words, he transformed me from sinner to saint, and although grounded for two weeks, I avoided the crucifixion of suspension and the lash of Dad's percussive lecture.

Please, do not misunderstand. I was not *only* in the business of breaking the rules; my conduct was more complex than that. Some teachers were taken by me, seeing something in me that I could not see in myself. My French-5 teacher, whom I had a crush on at the tender age of thirteen, would sometimes drive me home after school and talk to my mother about how much she liked me. Nonetheless, she sent me to the principal's office when I used a French cuss word in class when challenged to offer a word that the other students were unlikely to know.

My behavior fell on both sides of the moral spectrum. I did some bad things, but I was not a bad guy. I had a moral compass. I knew right from wrong. Sometimes I choose the latter. In this haphazard and undisciplined way, I fought to establish a sense of self in a world where I felt largely powerless and unseen. Undoubtedly, it was an immature and deficient sense of self, but far better than no sense of self at all.

At home, Jacques and I, born fifteen months apart and wedded together in time and a love-hate relationship, had developed an uncanny capacity to trigger rage in one another.

One memory of our sometimes bloody scuffles stands out from the rest. Jacques and I were fighting in the foyer when I landed a kick to his groin, sending him to the floor writhing in pain. Fearing reprisal, I raced upstairs, stopping at the top to see what he would do. As he continued to lie, whimpering on the floor, my mother entered the foyer and, to my surprise, responded with disgust to Jacques's mewling, demanding, "Stop laying on the floor crying! Get up! Stop whining!" To my surprise, as he lay in agony with no compassion found, a wave of empathy engulfed me.

My mother treated us differently. I do not believe contempt would have laced her voice if it had been me on the floor. In noting such differences in family interactions, I marvel at how parents shape their children and how the children shape them. Jacques served as a narcissistic extension for my parents: polished, handsome, and outgoing; he represented them on the public stage. Accordingly, as part of the unconscious training for this role, he was less likely to garner compassion for any perceived weakness while receiving praise and admiration for every success. I believe he internalized this experience. After the death of his wife of fifty years, Christine, when I asked how he was doing, he responded, "It's not as if I'm on the floor crying," perhaps unconsciously referencing the event that had brought him shame more than fifty-five years earlier.

Conversely, where Jacques reaped attention in worldly successes, my role was more thoughtful. My natural tendency toward introspection, fueled by the large heaping of isolation that characterized my life, fostered my role as an observer and fanned the world of my imaginings. Often described by my mother as thinking and feeling too much, I was labeled "too sensitive." My attention and approval were garnered in philosophical talks with Mutti and serving in the role of advisor.

This dynamic was so prevalent that it went unnoticed and unquestioned. In hindsight, I realize it was no accident that I was chosen to accompany my father to Heidelberg after his breakdown.

Throughout this time, my father's hand lay oppressively heavy upon us boys. From the day we moved into our newly built home in Annandale, Virginia, he put us to work as his slaves. He made us spend every weekend in the yard for over a year, including a snowy Christmas day. We removed tree stumps and brush and dug a hole for a rose garden like none other.

The hole was approximately four feet deep, twenty feet wide, and thirty feet long. We had to shovel the dirt out of the hole, sift it through chicken wire to remove the rocks and clods, mix the soil with peat moss, lime, and fertilizer, then put it all back. In the summer, we labored through the Virginia heat and humidity, suffering stinging flies and mosquitoes, and froze through the winter months. Dad, swallowed up by the deep and narrow well of his desires, was impervious to our protests. It is not that he did not care about feelings; only his mattered.

I resented him; we all did. This became particularly apparent one late afternoon as we broke out in sadistic glee when he nearly set himself ablaze. His was an epically stupid moment. The Great Man was smoking a cigarette, drinking one of several extra dry gin martinis, and engaging in another of his endless mind-numbing prattles as he poured gas on a large area of brush to burn it away. Blathering on, he fell ever deeper into the spell of his own voice, pouring gas the entire time. It occurred to me that vapors had to be spreading. A similar thought occurred to everyone else at about the same time. We started making eye contact and, without a word, slowly began backing up like synchronized swimmers, one small step at a time.

Eventually realizing that his audience had evaporated, Dad decided it was time to throw a burning match onto the gas-drenched yard. The gas ignited with a percussive whoosh and instantly transformed into a voracious fireball. The look on Dad's face was priceless: surprise mutated into alarm and alarm into a panic. In a split second, he launched himself into full flight, the fire biting at his heels like the hot breath of a yellow beast. We all noted that despite having run for all he was worth, he never spilled a drop of that martini. At this observation, even he laughed.

Countless times, Dad stole whole days from me, insisting I caddy for him as he played golf. On one such occasion, as I was seething with resentment over my lost day, Dad ordered me not to walk on the putting green since I was not wearing golf shoes. I wore tennis shoes and did not weigh much, but it was not my place to question, only to serve. So off we went for a day on the links with a couple of his golf buddies.

Midway through the day, we came upon a large green. Dad's ball had landed near the hole, about thirty feet from the green's edge. Standing beside it, Dad barked in a commanding voice as if addressing a mongrel dog, "Charlie! Putter!" not bothering to use sentence structure or the word "Please." Already simmering with resentment and now enraged by his debasing treatment, I instantly recognized that the moment for payback was at hand.

Let me walk you through it. First, Dad ordered me not to step on the green. Second, he demanded his putter. Third, I was not to ask questions, simply do as instructed. I sang to myself, *Oh me, Oh my! What to do?* There was only one solution, and I loved it. Slowly I pulled the putter from the bag, took careful aim, wound up, and flung it like Zeus slinging a lightning bolt. The putter, spinning end over end, sparkled in the sunlight like a cheerleader's baton, catching the attention of all present before hitting headfirst, and tearing a large divot out of the green, a couple of feet from Dad.

It was beautiful: he and his friends froze in a grand tableau, stupefied by shock and surprise. Red-faced with fury, stutter entirely forgotten, and mouth wide open, Dad screamed, voice rising to a crescendo, "Charlie! What the hell are you doing?!"

In a parody of a good soldier responding to his commanding officer, I promptly came to attention and dutifully reiterated his orders one by one in my best soldier-reporting-in fashion for all to hear, finishing with a flourish that made me proud, "Sir! Throwing the putter was the only way I could comply. Sir!" He was furious, but with witnesses present and at a loss for words, I had hoisted him on his own petard. Bam!

As far as my development goes, the terrain of my childhood was jagged and uneven. I was mature beyond my years in some ways and pitiably immature in others—I was a mishmash. The world around me did not make sense, nor could I make sense of myself, not knowing what I wanted or who I wanted to become. So, with no other plan in mind, I kept flailing around like a punch-drunk fighter, vaguely hoping that somehow, someday, someway, something would fall into place. I just had to keep fighting.

CHAPTER 9

College: First Try

I stumbled out of high school much the way I had blundered in, a year early and an education short. I barely had the grades to graduate. Going to college was not a burning desire. It was just the expected thing to do for a middle-class white kid, the next monotonous step in the long march called schooling. I had no plan B. The main appeal: I would finally be away from Dad.

I made it into Lynchburg College in Lynchburg, Virginia, home of Chapstick and Jerry Falwell, under academic probation and the requirement I attend summer school. The trouble with Lynchburg was that it was one of those rural towns that rolled up its sidewalks by 6 pm. Boredom lurked around every corner and was driving me crazy. In the fall, assigned to off-campus housing, my adventures began. My roommate was a talented guitar, harmonica player, and singer. He was also a babe magnet because he had 'the look'—tall, gangly, long-haired, and entertained at the local coffee houses.

One night, as we were hanging in our room, he pulled out a joint.

"Want to?" he asked as if he were asking me if I wanted to get free money instead of asking me if I wanted to get high.

Unsure, I tentatively reached for the joint, twisting it this way and that with my fingers, looking at it closely.

"I've never tried before," I admitted but felt no hesitancy in giving it a try.

He smiled at me, his eyes sparkling as if he were telling me his best-kept secret.

"Oh, you're going to like it. That's a promise."

And he was right. He introduced me to marijuana and then a variety of hallucinatory drugs. Before I knew it, a new world exploded before me—a whole other kind of education began. As the borders of reality melted away, my mind created new worlds of my imaginings. I was a quick study. Soon, while sitting on the ground in the backyard, I watched neon-colored dragons scamper playfully around the base of the dogwood tree, breathing fire in the brightly lit coliseum of my mind.

Another time, after ingesting hallucinatory mushrooms, I sat in the backyard for hours in a trance-like state. Coincidentally, wearing a red sweatshirt, I discovered to my delight, that red was a natural attractant to birds who, given my stillness, were not warned off. Ravens swooped down, beating their wings in the air just two feet from my face, their black eyes sparkling with life force as they wearily studied me. The pure aliveness of these moments sang to my being.

The hallucinatory drugs expanded the world of my imaginings, which I had always favored over the world of my reality, and now stood galaxies apart from the spartan confines relentlessly imposed in Dad's world.

I had not yet learned that it was one thing to be free and quite another to handle it. My grades plummeted, and eventually, the inevitable happened. Someone informed on us, and we were expelled.

My father picked me up from Lynchburg for the endless ride home, made infinitely longer by his lecturing and customary pokes, smacks, and slaps to the face as I sat trapped next to him in the passenger seat—I was starting to think my name was Curly. But I knew I had earned this treatment; my parents were rightfully upset. They decided I would work for a year to get my head straight before reapplying to another college.

That year proved inspirational, albeit tedious. I learned the limitations of job opportunities one faces without a college degree. The job was mind-numbing, and I knew with certainty that I could not tolerate that for long.

I worked in a government warehouse in Springfield, VA, which distributed medical publications. My job entailed walking up and down long aisles collecting books for shipment. I worked alongside African American trustees from Lorton Prison and befriended them, earning the nickname "ABC." When I asked what that stood for, they all laughed and said, "Ace, Boone, Coon."

By the time the year was over, I was desperate to return to college. My Uncle, Mac, knew the president of Baltimore's Loyola College of Maryland (today Loyola University), Joseph A. Sellinger. I was accepted under both social *and* academic probation.

I knew well that my life might have gone in a different direction if I had not had this family connection. I felt sorry for those without such ties and guilty for using mine, believing that I should have had to make it on my own in a fair world. But if there was one thing I knew about life, it was forget fair.

CHAPTER 10

Something Called Thinking

"What would you do if you were walking down a city street and came upon a drunk passed out in the gutter with one finger on the sidewalk?" This provocative question prompted several responses, ranging from "Help him up" to "Walk around him." But the craggy-faced priest, so different from The Priest of my previous acquaintance, was vexed by such pat answers, impatiently chiding in his Irish brogue, "No, no, no. You step on the finger!" Stunned, I was more than intrigued by his cruel assertion.

It turned out this priest was not cruel at all. As a recovering alcoholic, he explained: "It's a kindness to step on the finger. The drunk will grab any pretext to negate where he is; with his finger on the sidewalk, he will deny that *he is* in the gutter. The drunk needs to accept his reality to hope to change it." Thus, this priest introduced me to the problems created by denial and the critical importance of taking personal responsibility for your life.

To my surprise and delight, the Jesuits began teaching me how to think rather than what to think and introduced me to questioning authority, including the Catholic Church, more thoughtfully. Noting that the Church was the fifth wealthiest organization in the world then, they asked, "Why would the Church hold onto their countless artifacts and near limitless wealth rather than use them to help the poor?" Years later, while touring the treasures of the Vatican, I thought Jesus would have wondered the same. In such ways, the Jesuits were inspiring, modeling the importance of critical thinking and respectfully challenging the Church rather than echoing dogma.

The Jesuits also introduced me to various religions and philosophies, from Judaism to Hinduism to Buddhism, from existentialism to nihilism, along with courses in reason and logic. These disciplines stimulated my questioning mind and fostered a desire to learn. Never having applied myself to studying, I began learning how to learn. I started using as many sensory inputs as possible: reading out loud to take in the sound of the words, writing out key concepts to make a motor memory, and underlining sentences to intensify my visual recording of the information. Whenever my grade on an essay or test was disappointing, I borrowed the same from a classmate who had done well and compared them.

I developed strategies for taking tests. Ironically, this was prompted by my failing a test because I knew too much. I answered the first essay question in such depth that I ran out of time before addressing the remaining four. I learned to budget my time.

In another class, I recognized that the instructor graded by taking points away rather than adding them. Stumped on question three, I wrote the answer to question two at the bottom of the page, starting the next page with question four. I reasoned that the professor had to grade at least one hundred such tests and suspected that that wearisome activity would dull his wits, and he might not notice an answer was missing. I was correct.

Over my four years at Loyola, I advanced from a low C-minus grade point average to a solid B, missing qualifying for the honor society in economics by a tenth of a point.

I had chosen economics as a major because I still had no burning desire to light my way. Surprisingly, Dad gave me the best advice: "When you don't know what to do, keep going from minus to plus; keep marching ahead." Following this advice, I came to realize that learning is never a waste; everything relates to everything else.

Another thing I learned in my years at Loyola was the powerful warmth of unification. Having been in constant motion throughout my life, I had never had an allegiance to any city, much less a professional sports team. Still struggling with my sense of isolation and feeling uncomfortable in group situations, I discovered an unexpected source for giving me a sense of belonging.

One afternoon, I joined my fellow students to watch the Baltimore Colts on TV in the community room. Many students wore the blue and white colored jerseys of the Colts, and the anticipatory energy in the room preceding the game was palpable.

The game started, and the manic shouting began, creating a tribal enthusiasm that was contagious. The amazing thing was that the unmitigated passion and adulation for this team were not confined to students. It was statewide and knew no gender, age, or racial divide. On game day, we all became one.

As the teams played, I felt swept up in it, yelling raucously along with the rest. Screaming at the coaching, I shouted, "Jesus Christ, stop running the ball up the middle." "Do something more inventive." "Wow, what a play." Or, "Oooh! That had to hurt," when Mike Curtis put a hit on running back, or "That was incredible!" when Johnny Unitas completed a deep pass.

Every point scored was celebrated with loud cheers and high-fives. Every point given up to the other team was met with strident complaints and accusations: "It was a foul! Is that ref blind?"

It was the first utterly unifying experience I had ever felt a part of, providing a palpable sense of belonging I had never known. When the teams won, the whole state was euphoric, and when they lost, all despaired. Having been the perpetual outsider, I loved being part of something so primal that it cut through all divides.

When summer break came, a friend declined a job as a lifeguard at Assateague Island National Seashore and arranged for me to go in his place. Thus, as far as I know, I became the first legally blind (eyesight 20/450 with my glasses off) National Park Service Lifeguard. I could say they hired me sight unseen. Of course, this was not a problem unless I had to rescue someone. Then, whipping off my glasses, an optic fog would encompass me. As luck would have it, I never had to save anyone or, to be completely honest, not anyone I saw.

That job was a godsend. With it, I escaped Dad's enveloping presence. I reveled in one of the most exciting times of my life, absorbed in the physical challenges of lifeguard training, pursuing girls, and attending bonfire beach parties.

Yet, one event stood out from the rest. On this day, a Nor'easter was passing through, the sky seething with clouds. The 40 mph winds, along with the mountain size waves crisscrossing crazily and crashing into one another like locomotives driven by wild men, had swept the beach clear of people. I was alone; the rest of the lifeguards had returned to the barracks.

Taking in this vast spectacle, which filled my vision from horizon to horizon, I felt a need to join the cacophony that sang to my soul. It felt like a celebration of nature that was beckoning me to participate. I simply had to surf one of those waves or at least try. I entered the ocean with my surfboard, only to have sets of waves pushing me back to the shore. Time and again, I attacked the waves and, after numerous attempts, fought my way through the mountain range of incoming breakers. Fighting to catch my breath, I sat astride my surfboard nearly two hundred yards from the beach, just beyond the enormous break. I gathered myself while drinking in the power and tumult of the world of water that enveloped me as waves pounded like bass drums and the wind shrieked like cats flung through the air. I could only rejoice in the tumult.

I waited: First to catch my breath and then to catch an undulating mountain of water as it swept beneath me before morphing from swell to breaking wave. Each passing surge lifted me high and dropped me low like a child on a giant swing, my view of the distant shore blocked by the towering waves racing past, leaving me small and insignificant in the foaming, crashing bowels of the beast.

Rested, it was time. I began to paddle, quickly catching a swell that became a living thing as it shape-shifted into a wave. Tottering, I rose to my feet, begging myself not to fall, and managed to stand just as the wave broke, slinging me down the collapsing mountainside. I was riding the monster.

I thought, *Holy shit! It's high up here. Whoa! Going so fast, keep your balance! Don't fall!* That is how my self-conscious patter separated me from my instincts, slowed my response time, and sealed my fate. Down I went as the crashing wave jack-hammered me from behind, hurtling me from the mind-bending roar of the storm into the muffled silence and gloom of the world below the surface. Simultaneously the avalanche of the wave rocketed the surfboard high into the air.

Now I was truly afraid. Afraid of being hit by the board on its return journey to earth and of the unrelenting power of the waves driving me head over heels toward the ocean floor. I worried about a broken neck. Despite these myriad concerns, I knew to give in to panic was to lose, so I ignored the urge to fight the ocean, instead focusing on protecting my head and conserving my breath. On the ocean floor, the power of the wave partially relented, providing me with the time and space necessary to take in my surroundings.

Wonder soon supplanted fear as I became aware of the symphony of sights and sounds that now surrounded me. As waves rumbled past like freight trains overhead, a shaft of Cathedral light bore through the turbulent water, revealing the sandy bottom. There, rivers of sand and millions of sparkling bubbles swirled Dervish-like along the ocean floor, glimmering like sequins on a dancer's dress. Held in the ocean's firm embrace, rocked back and forth by the ebb and flow pressures of the waves trundling overhead, awe and an unexpected sense of serenity and beauty settled over me. I felt like a child securely held in his mother's arms.

I began to question myself, *Is this the bliss of asphyxiation?* but reasoned I had not yet felt starved for air. Reassured, I returned to the glittering wonder of the extravaganza that surrounded me like a million lightning bugs, my heart bursting with awe. Soon, a lessening of the pressure from waves passing overhead signaled an opportunity to return to the surface. I pushed hard off the ocean floor, moving from shadow to light, from muted sound below to the fury above, and fought my way to the shore, dragging myself upon where I lay as limp as seaweed.

The ocean taught me something about dealing with the power of natural forces, including human emotions. In later years, I learned to coexist with my powerful emotions rather than try to defeat them. I would sit with them, suffer them, observe them. I discovered that observing emotions creates a slight separation from them (observer to observed) and protects one from being completely swallowed up by them. Observing also allows the time and space necessary to reflect and learn from them. Observing emotion is the difference between having an emotion and being that emotion, between feeling panic and being panicked. Feelings, like waves, expand and contract, ebb and flow, and dissipate, given time. The thing one must accept is that it is typically not up to us to say when this will be; waves must run their course.

CHAPTER 11

Lottery of Life

T*hree-one-six, Three-one-six.* The number reverberated in my head like an auctioneer's chanting, "Going once, going twice, sold!" I was exuberant and felt like dancing as James Brown's voice rang in my head, "Watch me now!" and performed several tight spins before breaking out into Little Eva's version of "The Locomotive," followed by Chubby Checker's "The Twist," finishing with Elvis the Pelvis's signature thrusts. I was a dancing maniac—at least, in my mind.

The date: December 1, 1969, one month and twelve days before my twentieth birthday. I had just won the Lottery of Life. The selective service had conducted a lottery to draft men for the Vietnam war; my birthday was the 316th number drawn. Uncle Sam would have to empty America of young men before turning his baleful stare upon me; I had just escaped the Vietnam War.

There was one hitch: I had enrolled in the Reserve Officers Training Course (ROTC). Before the lottery, a single man, I was likely to be drafted. I first wanted to complete my college education and hoped the war would be over by then. But now, with the number 316, a new calculus was in play. I learned I could void the contract by quitting school.

Dad was not happy, but I did not care; he had not paid a cent towards my education. Then there was the Army captain in charge of the ROTC program with his in-my-face spittle-laden tirade concluded with, "You're not officer material anyway!" Impervious to his insult, I knew he had no care for me, just a quota to fill.

I enrolled in night school, where I discovered that it does not matter where you go to school if you hunger to learn. By this time, I was learning so well that the professor of economics asked me to teach the class when he had a schedule conflict. I was surprised since my night school classmates were older, with families and full-time jobs, some having operated in the business world for years and thus, to my mind, more qualified. Fortunately, the professor arrived early enough that night to save me from total humiliation. While trying to expound on various economic concepts, I stumbled upon gaps in my knowledge that paralyzed my capacity to teach. In this painful way, I discovered that if you do not understand something, you cannot explain it, and often, you cannot know what you don't know until you *try* to explain it. I would later realize that this is integral to how insight-oriented psychotherapy works.

After a semester in night school, I re-enrolled in day school. Although making progress, I was still far away from where I wanted to be.

My standard for success was Jacques. Talk about opposites. He was graduating from the University of Virginia as the president of his class and had been wined and dined by prestigious accounting firms, landing a well-paying position with one of the Big Eight in Atlanta. I was proud of him, all the while knowing I fell far short in comparison.

As I saw it, not only was that the story of his life but also my story. That was how things were, the way they had always been, and I suspected they would always be.

Upon graduation, I searched for work. It did not matter what; I still had no sense of purpose lighting my way. I had none of Jacques's polish nor air of confidence. Feeling every inch 'the country bumpkin,' I came nowhere close to landing a job. Dejectedly, I took a job at Merchant's International to run their import/export desk, arranging for the shipment of goods worldwide. That might sound impressive, but it was a clerical position, placing cargo through various shipping lines.

The latter, vying for cargo, invited me to Baltimore. Three sales guys took me to dinner at the Playboy Club and then to a strip joint on the infamous Block. At the strip club, everyone was solicited for oral sex and accepted. I might have accepted as well, but I did not have any money and feared that my Catholic guilt and discomfort with the whole situation would get in the way. So, I politely declined. The woman responded, "I didn't think so, honey, but I thought I'd ask." I imagined she detected straw poking out of my young ears.

In the car, after leaving the club, someone produced a joint, and shortly after, internal filters down, my enduring drive to understand things came into play, so I managed to suck the air out of the evening. Apparently, asking if they liked their jobs was not the way to go, especially when it turned out they hated them. I then compounded the problem by wondering how it felt to have oral sex with one woman while married to another. I wasn't judging; I was naïve. I was genuinely curious about how one navigated those rocky moral and relationship shoals. In other words, I was the worst of fools, the kind that does not know he is the idiot in the room.

That night, drunk and stoned, I stayed over at the home of one of the salesmen and woke the following day to a family breakfast. I met his classically beautiful and welcoming wife and two delightful elementary-school-aged daughters. While breakfasting with them, I could not help but think, *Why?* I thought about the secrets we keep and the primitive desires that skulk just below the surface. I was fascinated by the difference between how things look and how things are and wondered if anyone could honestly know anyone else.

Similar human dramas were playing out at Merchant's International. The manager, blustering, fat, and married, loved to show off his Masonic square ring, touting principles of morality and virtue, while flagrantly engaged in an affair with the Hispanic secretary. She, a full-figured woman, relished strutting about the office in stiletto heels, short black skirts, and tight white blouses, buttons straining to hold in her considerable charms while lording it over everyone else. I felt for her. She seemed unaware that hers was a moment of fleeting power on this smallest of stages.

That same manager kept stringing me along with promises of salary increases that, like mirages, remained just out of reach over the next horizon. Eventually, wising up to his deception, I quit and accepted a three-month contract as an accounting technician for the Department of Defense (DOD).

My workplace at the DOD was a cavernous room with rows of desks. Each morning, I marveled inwardly at the wooden faces of my co-workers that greeted me. Blanched by the unforgiving fluorescent light, lacking any sign of spirit or playfulness, these people were resigned to the drudgery of their jobs as necessary evils. They were so inanimate that I questioned whether they went home at night or remained frozen at their desks until someone came along and dusted them off each morning to begin another day, just like yesterday.

Almost certainly, their lack of liveliness was attributable to our work. A two-foot-high ream of computer paper awaited me every morning at my desk, each page laden with two columns of long numbers. My mission was to ensure that the figures in the right column matched those in the left. If not, I was to circle the offending digits. I had no idea what these numbers represented.

I became proficient at running a ruler down the pages, looking for any hint of deviance, like a sheriff on the prowl. Finished after a few hours, I would pick up a book, such as D.T. Suzuki's *Zen and Japanese Buddhism*. Some weeks into my job, the supervisor stopped by my desk as I was reading and asked: "What are you doing?" I thought it was obvious, so the question confused me. He elaborated, "Why aren't you working?"

"Oh!" I exclaimed, "I've finished." Then helpfully added, "If you have more for me to do, I'll be glad to do it."

Irritated, he said, "I don't have more for you to do, but you can't read a book. You must look busy."

I thought about this, then responded truthfully, "I'm sorry, but I can't do that. It's too hard. If you have more work for me to do, I will gladly do it, but I can't do "'looking busy.'"

He appraised me silently, trying to discern if I was disrespectful, and correctly concluded that I was neither rude nor insincere. He grunted and left without another word.

More weeks passed, and my contract neared its end. The supervisor returned to my desk, "We would like you to enter the fast-track management training program." He explained that this entailed intensive management training over six months and then exiting the process as a GS-9. I would get a substantial pay increase and more challenging responsibilities. I was surprised and appreciative, thinking, *This is a great opportunity, the possible beginning of a career. I, too, can be legitimate. I also can be respectable. Take that, Jacques!* But, as one part of my mind was thinking these thoughts, another was looking around the room, seeing these time-worn people doing their jobs day in and day out without fire or joy in their bellies. I then knew that continuing to work for the DOD would bleed me dry and not fit with some ill-defined vision I had of myself. I expressed my appreciation for the offer and declined. Two weeks later, I joined the ranks of the unemployed.

CHAPTER 12

Getting Lost, Finding Myself

I was unemployed but not alone. I met Jane through a friend. Smart, petite, pretty, quiet, and gentle, I was immediately attracted. We hit it off and moved in together three weeks later. We had been a couple for about six months when I entered the newfound freedom of the unemployed.

Following my usual planning, I decided to do something virtually everyone was against: go on a camping trip, not any camping trip but one with no end date or destination. Interestingly, although I could appreciate that this would do little in the way of career advancement, I did not feel I had a choice. Something unnamed but powerful was growing within me. Paradoxically, I sensed I had to get lost, to be free of external demands, to find myself. I knew I was drawing outside the lines, and I had no idea what form, if any, my scribbles would take. I was searching for something without knowing what that something was. All I *knew for certain* was that I needed the freedom to find *it* and would know *it* when I did.

Jane and I cashed out our bank accounts, paid the penalty for breaking the apartment lease, packed up my VW Beetle with tent and supplies, and drove out of town without a backward glance. My plan—yes, by golly, I had one—go until the cash runs out: go for broke.

I carried a gun. Everybody needs a gun. After all, we need to protect ourselves, don't we? There must be hordes of people, some of whom I know personally, who have required a gun for protection. Let me list them: hmm. In ten years, twenty years, thirty years, a lifetime, I realize I do not personally know anyone who has needed a gun to protect himself—unless you count war.

The headline-grabbing news strategy of "If it bleeds, it leads" unfailingly works angst into our collective hearts, leaving people afraid of the unknown or the unfamiliar, of people who do not look the same or speak a different language.

Everyone had been worried about our safety, including Dad. He insisted I take his .38 revolver. I wondered, *Was he hoping for a gunfight at the OK Corral? Another story he could tell, this time about his brave, and possibly dead, son?*

Jane and I camped on a treeless hillside outside of Atlanta, Ga., only to be awakened in the middle of the night by the arrival of several pickup trucks full of boisterous guys. Jane is attractive and the only female around; there is only one of me. Anxious about these fellows, my mind went into hyperdrive: These guys sound drunk. What if they decide to cause trouble? *Okay, I have the answer: I'll shoot the bastards. But under what circumstances would I do that? Someone telling a risqué joke or engaging in threatening talk or posturing? Or would it have to escalate to the laying on of hands?* Then there were other questions: *Where should I keep the gun so I could get to it? If I pulled the gun, must I use it, or could I bluff?*

I immediately began considering the when and how of using the gun, strangely forgetting that I had other options, such as my wits. In thinking about the weapon, I had gone from one to one hundred in a heartbeat. What had seemed like an easy enough decision in the calm light of day over a cup of coffee was proving difficult to sort out, startled from sleep in the dark of night. Here, fear intensified as the echoing sound of trucks racing off-road thundered across the previously peaceful hillside, and shadows, cast long by the bobbing yellow beams of headlights, danced ominously through the night. The raucous comings and goings blurred reality, fueling the boil of anxiety. If a problem arose, the chance of making a life-changing mistake was real.

Fortunately, I never had to answer those questions. Jane and I huddled in the tent until the guys finally departed. The experience, however, had left me shaken. I put the gun out of sight and out of mind. As much as I had played Wyatt Earp in childhood, the way of the gun was not my way; the gun was more a complication than a solution. I decided that in the future, I would only think of using it if I was already in trouble, not in fear of it. With that decision, I hung up my gun forever, and a legend was never born.

The next morning, we drove to New Orleans, where it rained for five days. Tired of waiting out the storm, we decided to push on to better tidings. Sunshine met us in Corpus Christi. We got out of the car and walked the beach, our spirits lifted by the lemony sun and the warmth of the buffeting wind frothing the Gulf of Mexico. Camping nearby, we befriended a couple from Pennsylvania and decided to cross the border into Mexico the following day. They offered to hide the gun inside the body of their van.

That afternoon, I walked the campground and spied an old, silver-haired man who, having just returned from fishing, was busy cleaning his catch. Catching my eye, he called out, "Why don't you come over and sit a spell?" There was something about this man that I could not identify that made me glad of the invitation.

I asked, "How was the fishing today?"

He responded, "As you can see, not bad. I've got some sea bass here, and that's pretty good eating."

As we spoke, he maintained a steady rhythm of scaling the fish, the scrape of his knife pleasantly joining with the dry-leaf rustle of his voice, creating a trance-inducing meter, like the use of a metronome by a hypnotist.

As he continued speaking, he called himself a snowbird, explaining, "My wife and I travel South during the winter and north in the summer." Laughing, he said, "We migrate with the birds."

He was an older man, and I wondered how long he could keep that up but said nothing. His bright blue eyes looked out from his sun-browned wizened face, exuding a quiet intelligence that otherwise was not on ready display.

Out of nowhere, a question arose from within me, "During those years of travel, is there anything that you learned about life that stands out from the rest?" After a moment's pause to consider my question, eyes twinkling in appreciation, while maintaining the comfortable washboard rhythm of his fish cleaning, he leaned forward. He looked me in the eye, "Of all the things I've learned in life, the most important is that ninety-eight percent of what I worried about never came to pass."

With those words, a calm descended upon me. I thought of all the myriad worries I had been wrestling with about forging a future and was suddenly, inexplicably, able to lay them to rest.

I left the elder behind that day but never forgot the soothing rhythm of his voice in song with the scraping of his knife and the lyrics of his melody. They ring as true today as they did then.

The following morning, we drove across the border. We had all heard the stories: tales of corruption, of police planting drugs, and of gun-toting soldiers extorting money. We had heard of drug dealers who would kill you and shrewd locals who would slide under your car, cut your fuel line, and come along later to "repair" your vehicle for a price. Soon our new friends, facing the unending barrenness and isolation of the land surrounding us, became anxious and decided to return to the US.

After making plans to retrieve the gun, Jane and I drove on. We crossed miles of desert landscapes, the terra-cotta expanses accented by flat-topped plateaus crouching massively in the distance. Even though there was little sign of human habitat, we came across people walking along the side of the road; women holding young children and men carrying machetes on their shoulders, causing us to wonder where they had come from and where they were going.

Gradually, the landscape changed, the road meandering among conical, treeless hills jutting into the blue sky, made more breast-like by the single shack resting upon their hilltops like wooden nipples. Jane and I were perpetually intrigued by a landscape foreign to us and a way of life only hinted at.

We drove forever south toward the Yucatan jungle and the Inca pyramids. Along the way, trouble finally caught up to us. In a struggling town, I turned the wrong way on a narrow, shadowed alley of a street. I had not noticed the faded blue arrow, painted on the corner of an aging building, pointing in the other direction. A young police officer, seemingly having hidden in wait, appeared out of nowhere, motioning for me to stop. He blandly pointed to the arrow, crouched down, and began removing my license plate. It took several moments for me to process what he was doing and only seconds longer for alarm to ring the bells of dread, fueled by all the stories of extortion, incarceration, ransom, and rape.

My head spun as fear and helplessness eroded composure, and terror took hold where calm had been just minutes ago. *What am I going to do? I can't let this happen. The longer I stand passively by, the deeper in the shit Jane and I will be.*

Panic coloring my voice, I demanded, "What are you doing?" But the officer did not respond, ignoring me entirely while implacably continuing to unscrew the plate. Thus dismissed, my feeling of impotence only amplified, I started yelling, "Stop, leave the license plate alone. Stop, leave the license plate alone!" my voice rising in volume, along with my growing terror. But the officer continued to disregard me as if my concerns were meaningless, as if I was meaningless, and our fate was sealed. *Fuck that! I'm not going down quietly!* No longer able to contain myself, I pushed him away from the license plate, repeatedly shouting, "El Capitan! El Capitan!" intent on drawing attention and adding another decision-maker in this process because this guy was getting me nowhere.

The young police officer, face turning red and eyes filled with fury, began to get in my face when a distant yell arose behind me. I turned to see a heavy-set, middle-aged police officer in the distance, a white hat with a gold braid crowning his head. The younger cop angrily pointed to the older, repeatedly jabbing his finger in that direction. I finally realized he wanted me to go to him. I asked, "El Capitan?" Irately he responded, "Si. Si."

As I approached El Capitan, the alley opened into a treed town square dotted with park benches upon which sat people chatting quietly, the scene brushed by the light of the late morning sun. In this tranquil atmosphere, so different from the claustrophobic feel of that dark narrow alley, my panic began to recede, and I could start to think rather than merely react once again.

Aware of the antagonism between Mexico and the United States, I decided that declaring myself a Gringo was not in my best interest. As I neared El Capitan, I called out in my rusty French, "Parlez-vous Francais?" He rewarded me with the beam of his smile. Thankfully, he said, "No," and, in jumbled English, asked me if I was French. I replied, "Non. Non. Je suis Canadian Francais." To this, he responded warmly, and as we spoke, he happily insisted that the guide I had hired several towns back was his cousin; apparently, this fortunate accident of fate made us friends. I certainly was not going to argue. After several minutes of amicable conversation, El Capitan, over the strident protests of the young officer, indicated I was free to go.

The latter angrily spat words at me as he followed me to the car. Shaken by the encounter and the angry policeman's continuing verbal assaults, I willed my rubbery legs to work the clutch well enough to put the car in gear and make our escape. The nightmares of my inner world had penetrated the nightmarish possibilities of the outer one and far too close for my liking.

As we moved further south, the landscape became increasingly lush, heralding our arrival in the Yucatan. Dripping with sweat in the humid air, the tropical bird calls and monkey cries echoing from the jungle, combined with the pyramids and ancient sports arenas, and the historical teachings of the guides all transported us to another time and way of life. After several days, curiosity sated, we turned north again, this time through the center of the country, on the way to Mexico City.

The rumors were partly true; there were gun-toting soldiers everywhere and even a metal pillbox from which a rifle barrel followed our every move in a local bank, suggesting that violence could quickly erupt. Nonetheless, except for that one police officer, the people we encountered were warm and welcoming, as curious about our culture as we were about theirs. Often, we laughed together, amused by each other's fumbling attempts to communicate as we took turns trying out words and gestures, like pantomimes: the entirely engrossing experience of adults at play.

Despite the richness of these experiences, the nomadic life was beginning to take a toll. Like any aging relationship, the new and novel were becoming ever less new and novel. I turned to reading more of the day, consumed by the works of Carlos Castaneda. As he recounted his shamanistic journeys under the hallucinatory influence of mushrooms, I was living mine, traveling along the same scorched landscapes and gazing up at the same star-encrusted night skies. Imagination stimulated; my eyes imbued my surroundings with color, wonder, and enchantment. I also stumbled upon the works of Joseph Chilton Pierce, who, like Castaneda, challenged the assumed order of reality and the nature of the extraordinary.

I had begun this journey to find myself, and now something that had always been there but I had barely grasped began taking form. This trip and these authors were breathing fresh air into my love of religious theory and philosophy, the power of spirituality, and the importance of living a creative and perhaps, sometimes—dare I imagine—even inspired life.

On the outskirts of Mexico City, my destiny continued to unfold: Our VW broke down. Stranded on the side of a crumbling road that wound its way up a desolate hill, Jane and I were at a loss for what to do. As we talked, a car pulled in behind us, and a lean Mexican man in his forties with short-cropped hair just beginning to gray, got out. To our delight, he spoke fluent English.

His name was Juan, and we hit it off immediately. Juan revealed that although he was a Doctor of Psychology, his work had become too administrative. In response, he gave up his practice and started a business servicing Volkswagens at peoples' homes; despite the loss in income, he said he was happier than ever.

I was impressed. A gentle soul and thoughtful man, Juan had the quiet courage to forsake his career and follow his heart's song. As importantly, this change was not a blind leap based on wishful thinking: he had turned his dream into a reality, the ultimate *realization.*

While we talked, Juan diagnosed the VW's problem: a broken alternator. He explained he would order parts, but their arrival would take several days. Then his inherent generosity shone forth when he invited us to stay at his Ranchero. Both Jane and I were thrilled. I was incredibly excited to have the opportunity to participate from the inside in the workings of a Mexican family.

That evening, sitting by myself enjoying a cigarette on the front stoop, an archetypal sight unfolded before me. Juan's one-story stucco ranchero stood alone in the middle of a vast flat field that stretched as far as the eye could see. A small farming village comprised of adobe huts huddled in the far distance. In the waning light of the sinking sun, women began emerging in ones and twos as small dots on the horizon, slowly making their way home, past Juan's ranchero, after a day in the fields. Silhouetted by the faltering sun, they moved as silently as shadows. As they neared, their faces, creviced by the relentless workings of sun and time and framed by dark shawls, were revealed. Slowly they trickled by, eventually disappearing into the distant village as the last rays of the sun winked out like a guttering candle.

I felt blessed as if I had just traveled back in time. This scene could have taken place hundreds of years ago, given there was nothing to indicate modernity.

After dinner, Juan and I smoked cigarettes in front of his ranchero, drank tequila, and shared stories late into the night under the sputtering light of a propane lamp.

By the end of the third day, I was ready to leave. I could no longer tolerate being in the house when Juan's wife cooked. Her food was delicious but seasoned with hot peppers fresh from the garden: breakfast, lunch, and dinner. By the third morning, the pepper-infused air brought tears to my eyes. I love spicy-hot food, but in Mexico, hot ratcheted up to a new galaxy of meaning. I had to get outside. The car was repaired, so we left Juan and his wife that day. As with so many memories in the making, that chance meeting was such a blessing and has remained forever with me. And why wouldn't it? It changed my life.

Upon returning to the US, the border patrol pulled us over for inspection. Ordered to empty our pockets, turn them inside out, and stand apart on the veranda of the station building, we nervously watched as they searched our car.

The search was exhaustive. One customs officer emptied the car while another circled it with a drug-sniffing dog. They examined the engine, removed the air filter, and inspected the manifold. Thirty minutes later, grinning triumphantly, the border guard approached holding a single marijuana seed between thumb and forefinger, saying, "I knew there was something," and let us go.

That evening, we became ill, Jane deathly so. She was vomiting, had diarrhea and fever, and alarmingly the slightest touch to her forehead brought pain. I suspected we had eaten undercooked chicken at a taco stand earlier in the day and were now paying the price.

This part of the US was indistinguishable from rural Mexico—there was no medical help to be found. So, I drove fifty miles across the desert before finding a clinic where relief was available.

We continued our journey several days later, pushing north across New Mexico into Arizona. Mile after mile, we drove on, seeing the Grand Canyon, the Painted Desert, the cliff dwelling of Colorado, the Rocky Mountains, and so much more. Each night, we made camp and enjoyed the dark skies so ballooned with glittering stars and streaked by meteors that the cosmos had to be celebrating. When the monuments of Washington, D.C., rose with the sun to greet us, we reached our destination: we had gone for broke and arrived.

By the calendar, we had journeyed for nearly three months, but to us, it had seemed like a lifetime. The magnificent sights and the surrealness of the whole escapade had transcended the limits of time, leaving a lasting impression on our lives. Though near penniless, we were happy. We had learned that everything could become routine, even non-routine. Now, wanderlust sated, I felt the need for a purpose-driven life.

During this trip, I had come to understand the paradox of freedom: I was free to choose among many options but was free only until I did—once committed, I was on a path. By the same token, if I refused to commit, I was also not free, destined as I would be to a directionless life. At some point, we all commit, whether we want to or not. I felt driven to dedicate myself to something and, for the first time in my life, had an inkling of what that was.

With the forbearing of Jane, the inspiration of Juan, Carlos Castaneda, Joseph Chilton Pierce, D.T. Suzuki, and the Jesuits, I had come to understand that I did not need a job. I needed a calling that sang to my heart and indulged my need to wonder about life and relationships.

A shell, almost unseen, had cracked, and I had fallen through to another world, a world I had instinctively sought but never known. I now had a destination in the twisting journey that had been my life. I was looking forward to the straighter path it promised; I did not hear God laughing.

CHAPTER 13

Waylaid

Something was terribly wrong. Night splintered into day—fragments of images coalescing then dissolving like phantoms. I emerge into a nether world, a succubus clinging to my face.

Awareness flares. Jane's voice says something about a car accident. I'm pulled under in a riptide of unease.

Consciousness returns. I'm in an ambulance, an oxygen mask strapped to my face.

Next, I am traveling down a white tunnel, fluorescent lights flickering past overhead, sounds echoing off the walls as the astringent smell of antiseptic burns my nose. I wonder if Jane is okay. I must have spoken out loud because her worried voice reached me from behind, "I'm okay. I just have a fractured wrist." I think, "*Just*?"

When next I open my eyes, it is to a circle of guys with ponytails looking down at me, one asking, "Who's going to do it?" I wonder, *what exactly is this thing they are so hesitant about?* before noting the long thick needle one is holding that instantly fills me with dread. My dread only festers as I watch each guy squeamishly try to avoid the task and worsens when I realize that these guys are interns who don't know what they are doing, trying to decide who will shove that thing into me. Done in by the never-ending recalcitrance, I blurt out, "For God's sake, somebody do it!" Embarrassment paints their faces, then disapproval—soon, the hard, cold quill slides in. Fluid pumps in, then out. Inflated, then deflated, I'm a human balloon, a sack of skin holding fluid and flesh together—the verdict: no internal hemorrhaging.

I surface to yet another squabble: "Who's going to hold him up?" Worry writ large on their faces; they are talking about x-rays: I recognize they fear radiation poisoning. One guy gruffly commands me to sit up, but my muscles refuse to obey. Another guy, resigned compassion on his face, grudgingly dons a lead-lined jacket.

I awake in a hospital bed, attended by a real doctor. I know this because his hair is gray, and he emanates competence and a professional demeanor. He says, "We're keeping you overnight for observation." Given that I am incapable of moving, I think this is an excellent idea.

It's the middle of the night, and something just woke me. *What could it be? Hold on, am I filling up again, or is this my imagination? No. Best mention it to a nurse.*

Minutes later, an aide shaves my torso and pelvic area, and then wheels clickity-clack as fluorescent lights flicker by overhead. I am being pushed along another corridor by an enormous black man in a bulbous green shower cap. It's been explained; I'm on the way to a major laparotomy, exploratory surgery. Dumbly, I obsess over the words "major" and "surgery."

Not wanting to be alone with my thoughts, I look up into the attendant's face and, trying to lessen my apprehension with human contact and a bit of humor, wryly remark, "Wow, this reminds me of a scene from General Hospital." He shows no sign of having heard me; rather, like a minion in the realm of Hades, he continues plodding along, staring straight ahead, stone-faced and unreachable. Finally, realizing he is not going to speak, I return alone to my dark musings when his stentorian voice reverberates in the empty hallway, says: "Yeah, man. But this is for *real!*" He then returns to relentlessly pushing me toward my fate. Doused with the cold water of reality, I think, *Geez, what a buzz kill! Does he call that bedside manner?* My sense of aloneness only reinforced; I recognize that *I am alone; I know no one here, and no one here knows me.*

An irrevocable truth strikes me during these cheerless musings: *I could be dead in a few minutes.* Having acknowledged this reality, I realize *I may soon know the answer to The Big Question: What, if anything, follows death?* A semblance of peace settles over me. *Whatever is about to happen is out of my control; I can fight it or flow with it—flowing seems wiser.*

Acceptance, and along with it its sidekick calmness, encompasses me,

October 22, 1972, at age twenty-three, I was waylaid on the way to visit my parents in Charlottesville, VA. I was napping in the passenger seat of the VW while Jane was white-knuckling the steering wheel, face plastered with a grim determination not to breach her edict: thou shalt never exceed fifty-five miles per hour. A car pulled out of a side road, and Jane T-boned it, later confessing she had frozen in fear and never used the brakes. From fifty-five mph to zero in a nanosecond—a hard stop by anyone's account. I had not been wearing my seatbelt.

Surgery revealed a fractured spleen; post-surgery is when all the fun begins. Split open like a frog in high school biology class, the incision held together by two hundred stitches, the outermost layer comprised of thick guitar-string-like thread encased in plastic tubing to defend against the sutures cutting into my flesh. Unfortunately, the tubing can't follow the line into my body. That is where the pain lives, particularly when I laugh, then my stomach pulls on the threads, turning humor into agony and tears of laughter into beads of blood.

Mucus gathers in my lungs, and pneumonia is a growing concern. The nurses pummel my back twice daily, trying to clear the phlegm while I protectively clutch a pillow to my stomach to hold my innards together. The physical sensation of bursting apart is so acute that one day, I adamantly refuse their ministrations.

Pneumonia has its way. With extra morphine coursing through my body, I enter the blissful world of Morpheus, amongst cotton clouds soft and reassuring, until the nurses force a tube down my throat into my pleural cavity. As I gag, choke, and fight for breath, the guitar strings tightly strung across my stomach shriek their terrible tune. The pain is excruciating.

I dread the nursing staff and their infinitely creative designs for torture. Time takes on a new dimension as I lay in pain on that hospital bed. Seconds seem like minutes, and days seem longer than weeks. Time loses all meaning; it is a vast, gray, empty void that stretches to infinity. I wonder, *How long I can keep floating in this expanse of unending pain. How long can I endure?* The answer is not hard to come by, however long it takes.

My family visits: Mom and Dad, Mark, and Michelle. Jacques and Ed fly in from Atlanta, everyone fearing I might die. During one visit, Dad whispers in my ear, "Charlie, I can see you are in a lot of pain. You can't hide it from me. But you never complain. I'm proud of you."

Several days later, Mark and Michelle visit, telling me that Jane, having been scolded by Mutti for having premarital sex, had left for Baltimore. I was enraged; what a way to treat someone when they are a guest in your home, especially as gentle and kind as Jane.

I called Jane to pick me up. Tentatively scheduled for discharge in a few days, I'm not too worried about leaving. All I know is I need to be gone before my parents return. I left the hospital against medical advice, armed with a prescription for Percodan. Thank God for Percodan.

My parents and I barely talked over the next several years. One of those rare times was to invite them to our wedding. They gave us three hundred dollars as a wedding present—no card. Jane and I bought the cold cuts and beer for the reception at her father's apartment. Unlike Jacques, who eloped to marry but still got a well-laid-on reception, Jane and I got nothing. We were citizens of the second rank, members of that lower caste, and there was not even a balcony on which to sit.

PART III

IF ONLY I HAD EARS TO LISTEN

I was breaking out of my shell and into my vocation. All along, it had been calling to me in the form of my interests and yearnings. My single regret was that I had lost so much time; if only I had had the ears to listen. My ignorance of myself had been profound, and now, as the veil lifted, I could only accept the costs as I relished the discovery. If there was one thing I was coming to understand, it was that we must each live our lives: there are no shortcuts.

CHAPTER 14

Asylum

Fortunately, this accident had the decency to bring gifts: a twelve-thousand-dollar insurance settlement after attorneys, plastic surgeons, and doctors received their cut. I could now pursue my education full-time and performed well—I had found my form of intelligence.

I have learned important things about myself since my return to Baltimore. I was an inveterate risk-taker, bull-headed, had a strong work ethic, was tunnel-visioned in my pursuits, and possessed a strong will to persevere. Once I had a plan, I saw it through. Sometimes I would get stuck, not seeing any way forward. Even then, I would keep plowing ahead until something unforeseen and unforeseeable came along, allowing me to break through the impasse and reach whatever was beyond.

As I doggedly pursued a master's degree in psychology, a troubling thought occurred: *What if I don't like working with the mentally ill? My love of theory was one thing, but the practice of psychology might be another. Wow! What a time to consider this. What if all the sacrifices Jane and I had made were for naught? What would I do then?* After all, we had been through, the thought of failing terrified me. It was one thing to follow my heart but another to cause harm to others in the process. With trepidation, I set out to answer that question.

I drove onto the grounds of the internationally renowned Sheppard-Pratt Psychiatric Hospital one fateful October morning in 1974. Not knowing what to expect, I was wide-eyed and anxious. I passed through a stone gatehouse and followed the wooded country lane across a rock bridge spanning a trickling brook. I then came upon a pedestrian overpass that led to a gazebo, both hewn from yellow wood and glowing golden in the morning sun. Slate-roofed stone and brick buildings designed by architects in the late 1800s graced the top of a hill, surrounded by expansive lawns adorned with countless species of shrubs and soaring trees through which columns of sunlight streamed.

Inside the main building, high-ceilinged rooms replete with oversized windows accented with stained glass infused the air with color and light. The windows opened to a view of staff and patients strolling the grounds and sitting on the Adirondack chairs strewn across the lawn, offering a silent invitation to conversation and reflection. The sounds of birds singing and bees buzzing floated through the open windows. I imagined well-dressed patients and staff mingling on the lawn enjoying high tea on a Sunday afternoon as had been the tradition decades past.

Grace emanated from this place, hinting at things seen and thought about in ways not common in the world rushing about beyond its borders. It was clear that Sheppard-Pratt had one purpose in mind—the care and healing of the human spirit. Sheppard-Pratt embodied the best meanings of the words sanctuary and asylum and promised a respite from a harried world.

I sat apprehensively before the Director of Volunteers. She described my assignment: "These are adult psychiatric patients on a short-term locked-door unit. They might stay anywhere from two weeks to three months." As her voice flowed on, the sound of her words receded as I thought about the varied implications of locked doors. *Why were they locked? Were the patients crazy? I mean, really crazy. Violent crazy. And what does crazy look like, and how does it act? Is it as portrayed in the old black-and-white movies? Wild-eyed, raggedy-haired people dressed in gray sackcloth, who will rise in unison to attack me?* My body hummed with these unasked and unanswered questions; I would not risk being refused a position because I was anxious.

Accompanied to the short-term unit, my escort rang the buzzer. Moments later, a nurse peered through a small, reinforced glass window set into the door. She smiled kindly and unlocked it. Like a swimmer entering the border of a frigid lake, I hesitantly stepped inside, the heavy security door clunking shut behind me with a tone of finality.

Alert to signs of danger, I looked around these unfamiliar surroundings, noting people sitting quietly alone or chatting together. Some looked depressed, others distressed, and some seemed perfectly fine, but nowhere was there evidence of any imminent threat.

The nursing staff welcomed me and explained my duties. I was to talk with patients, escort them off the hall, and otherwise help in any way I was willing. I will never forget my first case: a geriatric federal judge suffering from dementia and the loss of bowel control. I held his arm and took him into a bathroom with a showerhead and tub. He dumbly stood beside it, brown-stained pajama bottoms hanging limply from his bony hips. I fought the urge to gag as his stink threatened to chase me from the room. All the while, I thought, *How incredible is this? A man of such intellect and accomplishment rendered unable to think or remember in any coherent fashion, only capable of standing here, painted in his waste.* As I stood there looking at him, the harsh truth portrayed by his life threatened to crush me with helplessness: everything is vanity.

I talked to him softly, telling him what I would do before I did it. I gently pulled down his pajamas and rinsed him off with the showerhead, relieved when his waste released its clammy hold. Then I bathed him while speaking quietly, instinctively realizing it did not matter what I said, only how I said it. I shaved, combed his hair, and dressed him nicely in slacks and a shirt. Later, I watched as his wife and adult children visited him, their affection plain to see. I felt rewarded that they had this time together, their father looking more like himself with a vestige of his dignity intact.

I discovered that most of these patients are like you and me. The difference: they are overcome by psychological issues or deficits that render them unable to manage their lives, at least for a while. I could relate to this. I knew something of being alone in the world, overwhelmed, confused, disoriented, helpless, and needing time and space to sort myself out and discover a purpose for living. I also recognized the importance of having someone who cared about you in your life and knew that despite my lack of skills, that was the least I could provide.

I was interested in the patients' stories, how they came to be here, and what kept them from moving on. Their tales prompted my thinking about my life as I interrelated the personal and the professional, softening the division between them, the patients, and me. I came to see us all as fellow travelers on the obstacle course of life. I could not think of a more interesting way to spend a day.

The treatment team occasionally invited me to sit in on patient interviews. I cherished these opportunities. In my first team meeting, the service chief, Meyer Liebman, M.D., interviewed a young man awaiting trial for physically abusing his girlfriend. Afterward, Dr. Liebman shared his evaluation, noting what the patient had said, how he had said it, *and* what he *had not* said. He concluded that the patient, a voluntary admission, was only there to seek favor with the courts *and* one other less obvious thing: to become more skilled at controlling women.

I had always been a thinker, but these were exceptional thinkers. I had found a place where no thoughts were taboo, their value determined not by social niceties but by what deepened understanding. And, although understanding might be slow in coming, arrive it usually did.

In those first weeks at Sheppard-Pratt, I had the strangest yet palpable sense of being home. Standing in those moist lawns with a clear blue sky streaming radiant beams on that place filled with pain and sorrow and the nostalgic smell of petrichor, I would feel at home as I have ever been. I don't know how else to put it--It was as if in recognizing what was happening around me, I was finding myself in this place. It was not an experience I had knowingly sought; I had not known of its existence. I had fallen into it, and it fell into me like a spark laid to dry grass. Something within me burst into flame, a fire that would only grow in the years to come.

CHAPTER 15
Childbirth

Jane calls out in exasperation from our second-story bedroom window, "Charlie! What are you doing?"

It was a damn good question. What was I doing? I had no clue. It was patently stupid, but I could not help myself. I felt driven to complete the building of a fence to protect my backyard. *What was I thinking? That we were going to come under attack at any moment? And what was this need to plant a tree? I just had to plant a tree as if doing so was imperative, like raising a flag or marking ground I would defend against all comers.* I thought, *Won't it be great that our child can return thirty years from now and see this tree planted on the day he was born? Christ, what the hell is wrong with me? I am out of my mind. Jane's having contractions, and I am here in the backyard. Stop it!* Shoulders hunched, I took myself into the house and Jane's recriminating stare.

Years later, I shared this incident with a child psychologist. She laughed, "You Idiot. You experienced the nesting urge. You were preparing for your child in your Cro-Magnon way—no disrespect meant to the Cro-Magnons." Mercifully, it all made sense. Finally, I could stop castigating myself for what I had assumed were my selfish ways.

It was 1975, and I was twenty-six; Jane and I were still young and idealistic, and we would do everything *right,* certainly much better than our parents had. Jane attended La Leche meetings like a nun attending mass, and we opted for natural childbirth, at home no less, using a midwife. How perfect were we?

Long and arduous, the delivery did not proceed according to plan; we had to go to the hospital. We piled into the midwife's car; she and Jane were in the back seat while I drove. Her car was old and kept stalling. Irritated, I wondered why we had not taken my car but quickly realized that her car's backseat was much larger; she could deliver the baby there if need be. I drove faster.

We arrived at the hospital. I dropped Jane and the midwife off at the emergency room entrance. Upon my return from parking the car, I asked the receptionist for directions. She explained that I must wait until they called for me. I could not do that—the clarion call of impending fatherhood resounded within my soul, and I did not want to miss it. I explained that to the receptionist as the elevator door was closing. She seemed dazed by my explanation. Maybe she did not know what a clarion call was, or perhaps that an unshaven man, with tousled hair, and bug-eyed from a combination of exhaustion and adrenalin, was delivering these words. The door to the elevator shut as she dialed security.

I found Jane and the midwife in a supply room; the delivery rooms were occupied. Within minutes, which were both some of the longest and shortest minutes I have ever endured, Chandler emerged. Wet, tiny, helpless, and utterly dependent on Jane and *me*. Whoa, *Me!* It was a scary thought but a happy one all the same.

As I held him in my arms for the first time, a white-hot fierceness surged in my chest, incinerating all the nagging questions and self-doubts. I did not know how I would take care of this tiny monkey, but I knew one thing with certainty: I would.

For my parents, Jane and I were changed from water to wine, from last to first—a position of honor to which I was entirely unaccustomed. All because Jane got pregnant and gave birth to their first grandchild and *Grandson*. He was the Messiah, and Jane and I, by extension, held the honored roles of Mary and Joseph in the McCormack family. Now, there was always room at the inn.

Four years later, Keeley's born. Guess what? We were doing natural childbirth again. *Why not?* Bemusedly, I asked myself, *Hadn't the first time been swell?* But this time, we were delivering in a hospital. During delivery, I announced to Jane that the baby looked exactly like Chandler, then revamped my pronouncement as Keeley fully exited her mother.

As a proud 'all-knowing' father and training therapist with at least one course in early childhood development under my belt, I had spent months preparing Chandler for the arrival of this tiny Goddess of Love. I talked to him, drew pictures, told him what a good big brother he would be, and so on and so on—and then more so ons.

Finally, the momentous day arrives, and Chandler meets Keeley for the first time. As I watched over them, a proud smile painted my face as I felt full of myself for having prepared Chandler so well for this moment. In my finest *Father Knows Best* voice, I ask, "Chan, would you like to hold Keeley?" He assures me he would. Holding her, looking down in what I am sure is explicitly adoration, I intuit that he hesitates to speak, discerning that he is shy in the presence of this delicate deity. Feeling the potency of love in this *Golden Moment*, I encourage Chandler, "Is there anything you would like to say to Keeley?" He nods affirmatively, confirming the acuity of my perceptions. In the glow of the moment, I watch Chandler holding Keeley—*maybe a little too tightly*—as he stares intensely into her eyes. He then speaks in an earnest voice that brooks no misinterpretation: "I hate you! I hate you! I hate you!"

I am speechless. In the years to come, I would find that Chandler has the gift of rendering me speechless. Sardonically, I think, *Wow! That went well.* And then, trying to rationalize the incident, think, *At least it was genuine.* The realness is heightened only moments later when Chandler proceeds to pee on the floor in every room of the house. His message is clear. Where I had once felt driven to nest, Chandler is driven to mark his territory—so much for those classes in early childhood development.

Three years later, Caitlin was born. This time, we were not going the natural way. The first two pregnancies were breech births and very painful. Now, Jane unabashedly wants medications and plenty of them. Her transformation on this topic was so complete that I could imagine her donning a hard hat, waving directional flags, and calling out, "Back the truck-load of pharmaceuticals over here!" and then hopping aboard to help unload them. Somewhere along the road, the 'purity' of the birthing process had bleached away. Unfortunately, someone screwed up, and Jane did not get the needed medications. Then, birth was upon us. Once again, Jane gave birth au naturel.

Caitlin emerges, a bounty of dark hair helmets her alabaster face, creating so stunning a contrast that I spontaneously exclaim, "Jane, she's so beautiful!"

Chandler had now grown to the point where he cared little about another intruder into the family. Keeley, on the other hand, was beside herself with joy. She had just found a fun-sized doll to play with, and play they did. A fond memory is of Keeley and Cait, with a group of girlfriends, playing hair salon at a picnic table under the shade tree on a summer's afternoon. Keeley was chattering away while working on Cait's hair. Cait, then age four or five, chubby face set in a severe rendition of her role, sat patiently as the girls fluttered and gabbed around her, touching her hair here and there. The unself-conscious chatter of girls bonding reminded me of the excited chirping of birds. Thrilled by the liveliness of it all, I set up a video camera on a tripod and just let it run. I have no idea where that tape is today, but I do not need it. I can still see it all in my mind, fresh as the day it happened. I can still hear their tiny voices muttering conspiratorially; the words lost in the gentle breeze. I can still catch the scent of lavender drifting in the wind that billowed the girls' hair. And I still remember watching with alarm as Keeley raised her brush to smack an unlucky head.

Probably the smartest thing I ever did as a father was building a backyard pool. I cut down a sixty-foot-tall tree, scaling it repeatedly to trim its branches, then taking it down eight-foot lengths at a time: Paul Bunyan had nothing on me. It was a tedious, dangerous venture, especially when done alone. Stupid too, but at that time, life was good, safe, and assured, and I still recoiled from asking for help. I paid a heavy equipment operator to dig a hole and spent weeks shaping it with a shovel into a facsimile of a pool. Then I called a pool installation company to complete the job.

We spent the best time in and around that pool as a family. I taught Caitlin to swim underwater at eight months, and we swam for hours each week. Watching the kids swim was magical. Like cherubic angels, they flew in the depths of the crystal-clear water, happily flailing their tiny feet as their long golden hair, strobed by sunbeams, shimmered behind. It was mesmerizing. Their unblemished delight filled me with such joy that I was joy itself. Those were the best of times, some of the best of my life. Unfortunately, they were soon to end.

Throughout what was to come, these children were always there: growing, changing, needing me in ways I could not possibly have imagined and only partially understood, forever pushing me to grow beyond myself.

CHAPTER 16

Becoming a Psychotherapist

In January 1975, at age twenty-six, I was offered my first job at Sheppard-Pratt's Comprehensive Drug Abuse Treatment Program (COMDAP). My naiveté and idealism were staggering. On the walls of my office, I hung encouraging posters assuring that by working together with goodwill, we would overcome all problems.

I was functioning like a camp counselor. Picture me, strumming blithely away on a ukulele while staff and patients sit around a crackling campfire, the flickering firelight illuminating upturned hopeful faces as sparks leap toward the stars. Imagine the smell of roasting marshmallows perfuming the air as song and laughter fill the night. In cringe-worthy hindsight, I can imagine shouting, "Kumbaya! Kumbaya! It's great! You're great! I'm great! Everyone's great! And we're all so special. Don't we all feel better now?"

Now imagine I come to my senses and realize that the boy and girl scouts are streetwise, hardened heroin addicts, many middle-aged, and having done prison time. Some women, if not all, had sold their bodies for drugs. Envision what they must have been thinking about me. I dare wager it was not how lucky they felt I had arrived to save them.

Looking back on those times, I'm amazed by the grace and compassion those people had for me. They never mocked me nor made a face. It was not me taking care of them; they were taking care of me. I had been adopted and didn't know it. Even the medical director, Bill Abramson, M.D., one of the most scornful and scathing individuals to ever walk the planet, largely resisted the opportunity to belittle me. He would enter my office each week to provide supervision, take my chair (he loved those power games), and briefly cast a smirk at the posters but never say a thing. Later, he invited me to his home to bestow his grown children's old toys for Chandler. It was an uncharacteristically warm and tender moment, representing the ending of one era and the beginning of another. With this symbolic passing of a torch, I sensed he was grieving the loss of those sepia-colored times, the aura of which lingered on those well-kept toys.

The following year, there were cutbacks; my counseling position was reduced to half-time. Fortunately, the administrator, Carl Thistle, arranged to add a half-time research position. My job: track down the heroin addicts who participated in a program testing an alternative to methadone. I was to find and interview them to evaluate how they were doing.

The typical interview would go something like this: I knock on the door. A woman answers, her narrow face furrowed by lines of hard living. I ask, "Is Johnny home?"

Suspiciously, she responds, "What do you want him for?"

I do not know who she is, so I cannot say; I would be breaching Johnny's privacy. I tell her, "It's personal."

She looks at me with tired, weary, considering eyes, then shouts over her shoulder, "Johnny, someone here wants you."

A scruffy guy, T-shirt and jeans draped on a skinny frame, comes barefoot to the door, scratching his bed-head hair and rudely demands, "What do you want?"

The woman, who looks twice Johnny's age, has not moved. I guess she is his mother. But I still do not want to breach his privacy. I say, "It's confidential." He pauses a moment, considering, then says to the woman, "Sarah, go get me a beer, will ya?" She looks resentful but goes on her errand.

I tell Johnny, "I'm here to interview you for the drug-treatment research." Visibly relaxing, he opens the door and invites me in.

Contrary to expectations, the house is neat and clean. We sit in the living room, and Sarah brings Johnny a beer. Johnny offers me one; I decline. Johnny explains to Sarah who I am, and Sarah also relaxes. It is now becoming clear that Sarah is Johnny's girlfriend. Sarah then leaves the room. Johnny assures me he is doing fine, maintaining employment, and has no complaints about the drug l-alpha-acetylmethadol except that he misses the quasi-high obtainable from methadone.

And so, the interviewing goes, typically mundane by the end but often awash with undercurrents at the beginning. After dozens of interviews, I felt honored by these people allowing me into their homes and lives. In some ways, I was one of them, feeling far more alike than different. Indeed, these addicts were like you and me. Many held good jobs; their employers and co-workers never suspected a thing.

There were exceptions, however. One guy wouldn't allow me into his home, firmly stating, "No man! We talk out here." Of course, this made me wonder what he was hiding. When I told him that his urinalysis proved positive for heroin use and had resulted in his discharge from the program, he raged, "I'm go'in to kill you, you punk. You think you're a big deal, but you're not. I'm going to take you down to size, and you won't know when it's com'in. I'll find out where you live." It appeared to take every ounce of his self-restraint not to attack me right then and there. For all his considerable size and bellowing, he scared the heavens out of me.

Among many memorable moments, another stood out from my two years at COMDAP. It occurred on a snowy Friday evening. A couple, with three children in tow, appeared at the open door of my office. Clinic hours were over, and I was preparing to leave. The mother, an attractive blond with an open face, held a toddler in her arms. The other kids, girls, looked to be four and six. With beseeching eyes, she explained they needed methadone and a place to stay. Her husband, standing behind her, nodded anxiously in agreement.

What could I do? Didn't they know you can't just walk in and get methadone? Nonetheless, I couldn't let these people return to the snowy night. I explained the situation and assured them I would find temporary shelter. Remarkably, they declined. They knew more about the shelter than me and had no interest in going there. I marveled that they did not seem all that concerned. If it were me, I would be in an absolute panic. Hell, I was already in a panic, and it was not me. But they were calmly resolute, promising to return the following Monday before walking back into the cutting embrace of the winter night. I went home thinking; *I should have done better; I should have done more.*

Monday morning, the family returned utterly unfazed. They had found someone to take them in. What for me would have been a panic-stricken experience of not having a warm place to stay was, for them, part of the norm of a rootless life and nothing about which to get excited. Later, my naiveté and idealism worn down by the grindstone of experience, I considered the possibility that the parents had been playing me to get methadone and had always had a place to stay. Was it unkind of me to think that? Maybe. Or maybe I was growing up.

In 1977, at age twenty-eight, I was selected from eighty applicants for the position of Program Coordinator of SEPH'S Evening Treatment Program, a social support program for patients who worked during the day. In truth, it was a dull and lifeless affair; people were just sitting around. Worse, it was contagious. Soon enough, I, too, was sitting around, smiling the smile one has when their shoes are too tight. As I went through the same mundane and predictable routine night after tortuous night, I finally had enough. To quote Popeye, "That's all I can stands, cuz I can't stands n'more."

The psychiatrist assigned to the program, Steve Saunders, and I began taking patients into the community to restaurants and exhibits. I successfully made a case to the Outpatient Treatment Committee to allow patients and staff to have one drink, like a glass of wine, at a restaurant. I thought these were working adults and should be treated as such. We also invited people of varying talents, such as yoga instructors and art teachers, to share their knowledge with the group. We went on excursions, once watching sculptors make clay rise into vases as the potting wheel turned. Later, I would use this scenario as an analogy of spouses co-sculpting the vase of their relationship. The Evening

Treatment Program was thus transformed from a resigned march to lifelessness to vibrant adult get-togethers with people interacting and laughing with one another.

There was one problem. From the outset, I clashed with the program administrator—whom I shall call Ms. Glum, to protect the guilty. I do not know if she did not like me or perceived me as threatening her position. In any event, she had been crowing at me for months concerning the need to increase the size of the patient population. I did not see this as my responsibility. Mine was a clinical position, not public relations or advertising; she was the administrator.

Ms. Glum did not see it that way and was always on my back about it, although sorely lacking any suggestions as to what I could do. One afternoon, I was at the nursing station when the phone rang. It was Ms. Glum calling from her second-floor office. In a sharp, contemptuous voice, she reamed me out once again about the low census, concluding her scathing rant by demanding in a condescending tone, "What should I do with you?" Oops! That was it. I had had enough, and she had strummed the chords of my father's denigrating attitude.

At that moment, my McCormack Clan craziness poked out its head as I responded in a deadpan voice, dripping with equal parts challenge and disdain, "I think you should draw and quarter me and feed me to the wolves." At the time, I was reading a work of fiction set in England in the 1300s when this form of punishment was commonplace. My statement met with total silence and, I imagine, bewilderment. Holding the phone to my ear, I pictured Ms. Glum trying to make sense of the words so out of step with anything she could have anticipated. I waited and waited and then heard a click: she had hung up on me.

A month later, Ms. Glum called me into her office to impart *sad* news: "Charlie, I'm so sorry to inform you that we have to let you go. Because of the low census, we can no longer afford your position. Please accept this meeting as your two-week notice." Honestly, she did not seem all that sorry. However, she also did not look all that happy. Her look was like that found on the face of a toreador, carefully placing barbs into the bull to weaken him before the final sword thrust. She was not going to celebrate until the bull was dead. Then, I could easily imagine Ms. Glum running naked up and down the halls of the treatment center, well after closing time, manically laughing as she danced the Funky Chicken. It is an image I hurried to scour from my mind.

Stunned by this surprising turn of events, I left for home feeling a haze of fear and excitement. Fear that I had a family to support and no job; excitement in that I faced a challenge and an open future. The only clue that I was more discombobulated than I knew occurred when I could not find my car in the small parking lot. I looked everywhere before discovering it hiding directly in front of the entrance.

The following week, I received a call from the Outpatient Committee that oversaw the Day/Evening Hospital. The chair, Dr. Robertson, M.D., invited me to an exit interview. As the tiniest cog in the Sheppard-Pratt machine, I was surprised. *What could they possibly want to know from me?*

When I arrived for the meeting, I learned we were waiting for a final member: Ms. Glum. *Damn! I didn't know she was on the committee.* After a few minutes had elapsed, Dr. Robertson elected to start the meeting without her. "Charlie, we're sorry to hear you're leaving us. We invited you in for any thoughts or ideas about the evening program." His phrasing confused me, suggesting that he saw me as choosing to leave rather than being bum-rushed out the door. I probed, "Thank you, Dr. Robertson. I, too, am sorry that budget cuts necessitated the elimination of my position." Now, his face held a puzzled expression, along with those of the other committee members. That is when I knew the game was afoot.

Dr. Robertson explained that Ms. Glum had told them I was leaving because of conflicts between my work and school schedules. Wow! My appreciation for Ms. Glum rose ten notches. She had done a Machiavelli—straight-out lied to the committee and me. She would have pulled it off, too, if not for the fortuitous invitation to an exit interview that it was now clear she, too, had not foreseen. I assured Dr. Robertson that there was no such conflict.

At this point, Ms. Glum arrived, and Dr. Robertson questioned her. She handled the confrontation peculiarly: sitting stiffly, back straight, stone-still, and stone-silent. The silence continued, becoming increasingly awkward and uncomfortable until Dr. Robertson realized that Ms. Glum would not speak. Visibly unsettled, Dr. Robertson turned to me, "Charlie, I apologize for any anguish this has caused you or your family. I sincerely hope that you will choose to stay on." I assured him I would like nothing better and took this as my cue to leave. Ms. Glum never bothered me again.

Pretty crazy, but there is always plenty of crazy on the merry-go-round of life. It is, in fact, a crazy world. And why wouldn't it be? It is full of people, each flaky in their way, inflicting their craziness on others, at least until they resolve their issues.

CHAPTER 17

Man Plans, God Laughs

The night lay like a shroud over the dimly lit streets of the projects, the tinny sound of my moped engine echoing hollowly off its dreary walls as I made my way home from the University of Maryland School of Social Work in 1978, now age twenty-nine. The school was in one of the most dangerous parts of Baltimore. Shouts erupted behind me, immediately answered by yipping noises reminiscent of jackals feverishly tracking their prey. I looked over my shoulder, my heart turning to ice when I saw a gang of black youths shouting like Zulu warriors, running full-out, trying to close with their quarry—*me*. Mesmerized, I could only watch as the "warriors" maneuvered this way and that, trying to cut off my escape, effortlessly hurdling the obstacles in their path. Excitement writ large on their faces as each vied to be the first to count coup and divest me of my transportation, if not rearrange my facial features. Heart thumping, quickly understanding my role as the hare to their hounds, I broke out of my trance. With an immediacy I have rarely felt, I realized I must quickly counter the moves they were making, or my fate would be in their clawing hands. A wildly chaotic game of move and countermove ensues until I finally broke clear, giving my war cry as I jolted from terror to exhilaration: I had won, at least this night.

What made this experience exceptionally unnerving can only be understood if you have driven a moped. If so, you know mopeds are deservedly renowned for their lack of get-up-and-go—there is a reason they come with pedals. Indeed, it is not an exaggeration to suggest that they accelerate like sand through an hourglass. There was only one solution: once top-end speed is reached—twenty-five to thirty miles per hour—never, ever, slow down.

So, there I was, night after night, like a rolling stone down a steep slope, barreling through stop signs and stoplights, around and between traffic, and cutting corners to avoid slowing down, all with little regard for what lay ahead, but fully aware of what followed behind.

Though the "warriors" never caught me, there were some close calls. Ironically, the most significant came when I had left the pursuing gang far behind and stopped for a red light. Given the better lighting, denser traffic, and random police patrols at the corner of North and Charles, I was not worried about the gang. Still, I kept a vigilant eye—this area of town was also infamous for its crime. So, there I sat, waiting patiently for the light to turn green, enjoying the gentle breeze of warm air caressing my skin and the smell of cooking hamburgers wafting over from the White Castle restaurant situated on the corner when out its door stepped a predator.

Immediately, I knew he was a shark. Just as I quickly recognized him for what he was, he instantly recognized me for what I could be: his prey. Maybe in his thirties, sporting a garish gold chain and red baseball cap planted askew on his head, he had instantly begun scanning his environment, his eyes passing over me before jerking back in an almost comedic double-take. Fear tightened my chest as he swaggered towards me, a wolfish rictus contorting his face. The sights and sounds of the city faded as I focused on the incoming threat.

"Was' dat you ridin'?" asked the shark cheerfully. We could have been long lost buddies except for his hard, scarred face and dead fisheyes gave the lie. Time was on my side—a squad car could roll by at any moment—so I did my best to put off the confrontation, going along with the pretense that we were shooting the shit.

"It's called a moped; they are used all over the world." He pretended interest as he walked around the bike. Then, head tilted quizzically, and with brotherly camaraderie, he said, "Get off da bike. I tries it out," ridiculously implying that he would take it for a spin and bring it back.

Understanding that any trace of fear or indecision would only encourage him, I dryly responded, "That isn't going to happen." He froze into place, staring at me silently, dead fisheyes coldly assessing, waiting for me to fold.

What he did not know was that I could take a beating with the best of them. After several thunderous heartbeats, he realized I was not getting off that bike. Angered, he barked, "What if I jus shoot you in da hed and takes' it?" I did not see a gun, but he could have easily concealed one in his loosely hanging sports jersey. That strange feeling, again unbidden, came over me, that quiet sense of acceptance and resolve and a tentative curiosity to see how this would play out.

Nonetheless, whatever ensued, I knew one thing was certain: I was not getting off that bike. I responded quietly, matter of factly, without challenge or braggadocio, "You gotta do what you gotta do. I gotta do what I gotta do."

He stood silently, surprise and curiosity flickering behind his eyes. After a short time assessing the situation, he broke the stand-off with a bark of a laugh and said, "You aw-rite. I jus kiddin'." He turned and walked away, disappearing into the night from which he had come.

Such is life, as capricious as the weather, fickle in ways beyond anyone's ability to foresee or control. Though my life sometimes seemed—and seems—on track, I know things can fall apart in a nanosecond. My tumultuous childhood was reason enough to see the truth of this. Indeed, such things happen to everyone with enough regularity to give rise to the Yiddish saw, "Man plans, and God laughs."

One such event landed me on that moped, careening through the projects. I had been pursuing admission to a doctoral program in psychology, confident that I would be a desirable candidate. To ensure this, I applied to twenty schools and then sat back to wait for the acceptances to start rolling in. However, rejections were all that followed. The worst part was that I did not understand why and fell back on an explanatory concept in keeping with my insecurities: I deduced that these schools had recognized my underlying inadequacies. Then one day, a letter arrived that gave reason to my plight. It stated that I did not qualify for admission with only six credits in psychology.

I was dumbstruck. I have a master's degree in psychology. I instantly realized that Loyola had sent out partial transcripts. Perhaps my random shifts from day school to night school and back again, or from part-time to full-time student, had created an archival complexity that invited mistakes. In the end, however, the cause did not matter. Loyola's oversight was a fatal blow to my ambition to become a psychologist. Even with my bullheadedness, I could not imagine putting my family's needs on hold for another year. I accepted this bitter pill and thought about my options. My ambition to become a psychologist was not to be, but the more bedrock desire to become a psychotherapist was still within reach. At Sheppard-Pratt, I discovered that unlike the master's degree in psychology, a master's in social work offered the license to practice psychotherapy.

That is how, in 1978, at the age of twenty-nine, I entered the two-year master's program at the University of Maryland School of Social Work. I put in eighty-plus-hour work weeks for the next two years. A hardship for me but even more difficult for Jane burdened with taking care of Chan in my absence. Jane had become a teacher, and a good one, receiving stellar performance evaluations. I was proud of her more than she was of herself, given her need to be perfect in whatever she did. Though highly regarded, Jane left teaching, too burdened by the stress of trying to meet her perfectionistic standards. She took less demanding secretarial jobs with a temporary agency. Ironically, in this capacity, her intelligence still shone through. Within two years of temping with Meals on Wheels of Maryland, she became its Acting Director.

Nonetheless, I was determined to get my license as quickly as possible, driven by an intense desire to put the hard financial times behind us.

I graduated with a Master of Social Work on January 13, 1980, my thirty-first birthday. In a couple of months, I would be a licensed psychotherapist. Life had presented unanticipated obstacles, and like most people, I had learned to adapt, sometimes stepping back to get ahead but never losing sight of my goal.

CHAPTER 18

Power???

Our home life was good. We took thousands of photos and hours of videos, made love with some regularity, and argued upon occasion. However, with the arrival of kids, all this started to change. When our second child, Keeley, was born in 1979, we agreed Jane should be a stay-at-home mom.

As time passed, Jane grew ever more child-centric, preparing a different meal for each of the kids in a futile effort to avoid their complaints and insisting on going to Disney World every day for a week without taking any time to enjoy the beach. To me, this spoke to her need to provide her children with what she thought would give them the happy childhood she had never known and, importantly, to lessen any childhood complaints that might stimulate the negative feelings that linked her to her ever-critical and abusive mother. Jane thus fell victim to parenting for the good feeling—the approval of her children—to avoid feeling like a bad mother, to avoid being her mother.

As for me, with a master's degree in Social Work securely in hand, along with three years as the Program Coordinator of Sheppard-Pratt's Evening Treatment Program, I felt the need to expand my clinical horizons. Fortuitously, a family therapist in the Day Program wanted to make a change. Ta-da: I transformed into a family therapist with the business cards to prove it.

As the weeks passed, I grew into my new job. In some ways, it felt familiar, harkening to my role in my family of origin. Still, I was becoming ever more knowledgeable about how little I knew. Each day, I learned to appreciate the uncomfortable truth that graduate social work programs cover a wide variety of topics but specialize in none. The nine credit hours I had completed in the theory and practice of family therapy had not prepared me for the shifting complexities presented by a single family, much less many different families, each of whom posed an ever-mutating challenge to my efforts to help.

Feeling my inadequacy, I signed up for a workshop conducted by Bill Silver, DSW, a faculty member of the famed Philadelphia Child Guidance Clinic, on Structural Family Therapy (SFT). The workshop was well-attended, and the auditorium was abuzz with conversation as we waited for Dr. Silver's arrival; he was ten minutes late. Finally, rushing, he entered the auditorium disheveled and wrestling with a jumble of files that threatened to spill from his arms with every jagged step. Already the poster child for overwhelmed and disorganized, he tripped on the stairs to the stage, launching the files across the floor. The audience gasped, and nearby attendees jumped to the rescue.

Files clutched afresh in his arms, Dr. Silver completed his unceremonious journey to the podium. There, he transformed and used his dramatic entrance and the assembly's rescuing response to illustrate how the group rewarded dysfunctional behavior. He pointed out that it was his job to be on time, organized, and prepared, yet here he was, none of those things, and we were showering him with concern and care.

From there, Bill used storytelling and video clips to illuminate the theory of SFT. His ideas were new and heady stuff. I might even say empowering, given that that was the buzzword of the workshops of that era. He certainly had me excited by the promise of mastery and competence that thus far had eluded me.

Consequently, I formulated a plan to acquire such training. I could ill afford the time or money to travel to Philadelphia, so I decided to bring the program to me. Sheppard-Pratt agreed to provide a meeting room, video recording equipment, and a one-way vision room. The participants would pay Dr. Silver. He was receptive to the idea, and in 1981, eight of us began meeting for three hours every other week, a practice that would continue for the next three years.

It was an exciting time: learning theory, applying theory to practice, analyzing videotapes of sessions, receiving live supervision from Bill via phone from behind the one-way vision mirror, and even having Bill join the presenting therapist with the family to demonstrate in real-time how a master therapist works. I learned how the organization of the family, its hierarchies and structures, could create pathology and how changing those structures could help alleviate the problem. I studied the importance of observing patterns of interactions that unfolded like a dance within each family and how to create paradoxical interventions to disrupt these sequences so that the family would become more amenable to grasping new, healthier forms of organization. For example, in a family structure that fostered enmeshment and dependency, I would prescribe that the parents and the identified patient spend all their waking hours with one another so that the enmeshment became so burdensome that the family would revolt against the prescription, thus moving toward separateness.

I learned about field theory, sub-groups, triangulating communications, and shifting family alliances, which supported the continuation of the problem the family was encountering. I studied the tendency for family members to exchange roles, providing the illusion of change while maintaining the same dysfunctional family patterns. For example, if the identified patient improved, a different family member would become problematic. Such shifting roles, managed by an unskilled therapist, would result in the focus of attention careening from one family member to another while leaving the dysfunctional family structure unchanged.

Over time, Bill validated me as a skilled therapist, lauding to the group my willingness to "go where even angels fear to tread," and predicted that I would publish professionally.

I learned a lot from structural family therapy. I interwove its behavioral focus with the more insight-oriented approach that came naturally to me, given my ever-present drive to understand. Sarah's story stands in illustration. In her early thirties, round of face, and brown hair hanging limply to her shoulders, she was plain in grooming and appearance, perfectly fitting the prototype of a person with a deeply conservative and religious upbringing. She carried about herself an aura of feminine strength and grace. I liked her immediately.

Sarah came to the hospital in a state of voluntary mutism, thus making verbal therapies difficult, if not impossible, to implement. She had refused to speak for nearly a year while secluding herself in her parental home. A previous inpatient effort had proved futile; the family was desperate. She talked to no one and did her best to avoid all human contact.

Faced with this challenge, I began meeting with Sarah and her parents in family sessions, thinking maybe she would not talk, but her parents would. The parents, slightly built and carrying the gray hair of their late sixties, were soft-spoken with intelligent eyes. Of deep faith, they were not given to excesses of any kind, dressing and carrying themselves modestly. They were willing to try anything that would help. So, one late morning, with the sun streaming through the window, we all gathered in Sarah's room since she refused to leave it.

Sarah lay unmoving on her bed, feigning sleep. Without paying her the slightest mind, I moved chairs in, and once everyone was seated, spoke with her parents about family life: history, how they met, and what life was like with Sarah growing up, all while Sarah silently ignored our presence, as I ignored her. She wasn't the only one who could ignore other people.

About twenty minutes into this pleasant conversation, I noticed Sarah starting to move about in mild agitation: Something was brewing (yet she had not been called upon to do anything). A few minutes later, my suspicion was confirmed when Sarah began making guttural noises. Encouraged, we all looked at her in askance, but her face remained hidden, facing the wall away from us. Sarah's mother asked, "What is that you're saying, Dear? We can't hear you?" Sarah then spoke, "Shut up! I hate you! Liars." These were the first words Sarah had spoken in over a year. Confusion and embarrassment worked their way across the mother's face while the father displayed puzzled concern. Such words did not reconcile easily with their view of themselves. The mother leaned forward, hopeful, and said, "What do you mean, Dear?" Sarah fell back into a reproachful silence. Then, minutes later, as the family meeting continued, Sarah repeated: "I hate you! Liars!" When I asked what she was referring to, I was ignored and left feeling like a rude interloper rather than a helping professional.

Several weeks passed with twice-weekly family sessions in which Sarah would repeat her words. But there had been other changes as well. She was now sitting up in bed, scowling at her parents. Then, Sarah upped the ante. She climbed out of bed and began pacing, keeping as far from her parents and me as she could. After some minutes of this disturbed meditation, she halted, stood still, and tilted her head to one side as if in silent conversation with herself.

Coming to a decision, Sarah began moving towards her parents in a bizarre, slow-motion, stutter-step kind of way, like a person tentatively testing the strength of the ice upon a pond. In this cautious fashion, she slowly approached her parents and then began swatting at them. It bordered on the slapstick, for she had arrived several inches short, resulting in her hands flailing ineffectually in the air. After several failed tries, Sarah readjusted her position and began slapping her parents on their arms and legs, her assault so feminine and restrained that I felt little apprehension.

Sarah's father, spine stiffening, raised his arms to fend off the hits. Her mother seemed torn between a desire to move towards Sarah to comfort her and the wish to pull away. After thirty seconds of observing this puzzling interaction, I intervened, physically wedging myself between Sarah and her parents without touching her. Gently, almost apologetically, I told her I could not allow her to keep hitting her parents. Sarah briefly looked at me, quickly dismissed what she saw, and immediately went for them again. As I once more put myself between them, one thing became clear: Sarah wanted no physical contact with me. Thus, as I repeatedly countered each of Sarah's efforts to go around me, we came to dance a silent samba of approach and avoidance.

Over the following sessions, Sarah's attacks on her parents continued, yet she would slap at them rather than use her fists—not the actions of a person who wanted to do serious harm. What also stood out was that her parents did little to defend themselves. They would turn toward her and hold their arms up to ward off her slaps but did nothing to pull away or restrain her. They did not even ask her to stop, perhaps fearful of losing this hard-won contact. Still, the intensity of Sarah's attacks was escalating, and my role as a bodyguard was wearing thin, so I recruited a mental health worker, Rob, to join me. His assignment? To protect Sarah's parents when I asked him to but never cause Sarah to feel subjugated or overpowered in any way.

Behavior communicates. It has intentionality that may reveal underlying motivations. My challenge was to figure out what Sarah's motivations and intentions were, not to change her behavior. What was she trying to express? What was she trying to initiate? For reasons that eluded me, I intuited that it was essential for Sarah that her parents engage more fully with her. I wondered if the more brutal slaps arose out of frustration that they had not done so. To this end, I instructed them to restrain Sarah by wrapping their arms around her and holding her tight (behavioral intervention). I asked Rob only to intervene if Sarah got the upper hand.

As a result, Sarah and her parents now had lots of intense, no-verbal, physical contact. The parents would push Sarah back onto the bed, where they would wrap themselves around her arms and legs and hold on tight. By the end of each session, Sarah would lie panting and exhausted, held in her parent's arms. Sarah's mother embraced Sarah's upper torso with her front to Sarah's back while Sarah's father had her legs. In this position, Sarah lay exhausted, head lolling onto her mother's chest, who used each such opportunity to stroke her hair gently. They painted a beautiful picture of a loving mother comforting her child.

Over the weeks that followed, Sarah became less physical and more vocal. She was now speaking, sometimes in complete sentences. Consequently, I began meeting with her individually several times weekly—in addition to the family sessions—in service of developing our relationship and the pursuit of understanding. Slowly, Sarah revealed she had worked for the Peace Corps and became pregnant out of wedlock in a remote area of Brazil. Hers was a strict religious family, and her parents and church responded to her pregnancy by avoiding the topic (i.e., not engaging): Sarah felt silently judged. When she later miscarried, she also felt condemned by God. That is when, feeling shunned by the world, she began shunning the world, an act of defiance in service of the survival of the self to which I could relate.

Sarah and I talked about her pregnancy, the father of the child, what had happened to that relationship, her feelings about her miscarriage, and the difficult weeks of fear and isolation before returning home from Brazil. What was changing now? Why was Sarah coming out of her burrow? I had my ideas. To me, the caring and touch of her parents, their unwavering willingness to participate week-in and week-out in these challenging sessions, and their desire to hold and comfort her were felt by Sarah. As Sarah's rage ebbed, she began accepting their care and rewarded them by haltingly putting her feelings into words, words her parents were now willing to hear. They had lost their daughter for a time and now understood why. They were not going to make that mistake again.

Several months later, Sarah was discharged from the hospital and, after a short outpatient stint, moved to California. Many months later, I received a letter from Sarah thanking me for "not giving up" on her and relating that she had completed a master's degree in bilingual education and worked with the Hispanic community. She had gone from being without spoken language to speaking two and helping others learn to speak them as well.

Even though I was able to interweave SFT with my insight-oriented need for understanding, the biggest thing I learned over those three years of training in SFT was this: SFT, along with its behavioral interventions, offered helpful tools, but as a stand-alone therapy was not for me; it lacked the drive to help people understand themselves that I think is necessary to growth and enduring change. In the structural approach, there was little valuation of the importance of understanding someone—his heart, soul, or motivations—nor of an authentic relationship between therapist and patient. The therapist did things strategically to affect the way family members related to one another—presumably from his position of superior wisdom. I did not like the feel of manipulation, presumption, and arrogance, attitudes that seemed to go together with the pursuit of therapeutic "empowerment."

The last problem and the most crucial was it did not work. In the short term, patients and families would change their behaviors, but significant regressions soon followed. I saw two reasons for this. One: the therapist eventually lost credibility because the manipulative nature and lack of authentic connection were felt, even if not named, by the family. And two: the change was built on something exterior to the person—observable behavior—rather than something interior, i.e., the way people saw, thought, and felt about things. SFT relied on the premise that if you can change a family's behavior, the psyche (if the existence of such an entity was even granted) would follow. It sounded good; it just did not work that way. To me, this only made sense: if the pathological needs of people went unaddressed, the likelihood of any change in behavior enduring was minimal, relying as it would on the finite resource of will rather than want.

Not knowing what else to do, I decided to plunge deeper into the human condition to better plumb its mysteries and applied for a job as a clinical social worker on Unit B-2, a locked-door, long-term adult psychiatric inpatient service. Here, I would be treating the sickest of the sick and get introduced to a different treatment approach, one far more complex and thought-provoking. What I did not anticipate was that it would turn me inside out in ways that I could have never foreseen or imagined.

CHAPTER 19

The World Gone Crazy

I started working in B-2 in 1982, at age thirty-three. Within days of beginning my work, I was wondering, *What have I gotten myself into?* These patients were suffering from a word-salad of major disorders manifested at their most extreme: depression, bipolar disorder with and without psychotic features, dissociative disorder (at that time known as multiple personality disorder), eating disorder, narcissistic and borderline personality disorders, and schizophrenia.

Many patients were suicidal, and some were homicidal. One woman, the mother of two, self-enucleated an eyeball, literally interpreting the biblical injunction, "If thine eye offends thee, pluck it out, and cast it from thee." A twenty-year-old girl jumped seven floors from a parking garage and survived. She was now suffering the ongoing anguish of her severely broken body and festering regret. Yet another woman drowned her three children during a psychotic episode to "Save them from the Devil." Imagine that. How does anyone come to grips with the horror of murdering their children once psychosis lifts?

These are tales of human tragedy with a capital T. Such suffering was not the kind touched by so-called empowered therapists. After all, what therapist would be so arrogant as to assume the all-knowing mantle of power in the face of such grisly life-and-death realities? What reward could entice a fundamental change in a compelling wish to die? What extraordinary gift would allow a therapist to "fix" a person in the devastating aftermath of a psychotic desire to kill?

Sheppard-Pratt was famous for treating the troubled among the troubled, often providing the last hope for patients who had experienced multiple failed inpatient treatments elsewhere. They came from Asia, Europe, and Latin America, as well as across the United States and Canada. When I arrived on B-2, the staff equated social work with handing out benefit checks and serving as a family liaison/discharge planner, none of which held the slightest appeal to me. Also, B-2 was psychoanalytically oriented, concerning the workings of the human psyche and forces not visible to the naked eye, just opposite SFT. I had little knowledge of psychoanalytic theory and thus, once again, found myself starting over from scratch, learning a new culture and a new language: I feared I had made a colossal mistake.

Attending my first treatment team meeting, I observed Dr. Klement, M.D., B-2's service chief. Austrian, her English heavily accented, her bearing queenly in the best sense of the term. She sat tall and austere, thinning black hair coiffed, back ramrod straight—regal without effort or pretense, one of those rare people whose poise never faltered whether in the face of turbulent seas or mutinous crew. In the years ahead, despite the life and death dramas that surrounded us, she remained above the fray, maintaining perspective, never becoming reactive or raising her voice, her hand ever-steady on the rudder of the treatment team.

The chairs surrounding her, forming the necklace to her focal stone, were occupied by gems in their own right. Clarence Schulz, M.D., author and senior training psychoanalyst for the Baltimore/Washington Psychoanalytic Training Program; two psychiatrists, one from Mexico, Dr. David Gonzalez, and one from Wales, Dr. David Cowie; and a psychiatric resident, Dr. Roger Lewin, a graduate of both Harvard and Yale, who would author several books in the coming years. Rounding out the team was a post-doctoral fellow in psychology, Denise Forte, whose husband was the medical director of Chestnut Lodge, a famous psychiatric hospital outside of Washington, D.C.

But that was not the end of it. A potpourri of nurses, art therapists, dance therapists, occupational therapists, and mental health staff with decades of experience and hard-earned wisdom augmented the team.

Viewed through the eyes of a guy who had barely made it out of high school, was kicked out of college, and had a less-than-stellar career in business, followed by an even more humbling tour as an auto-body man and mechanic, this was heady stuff. As I looked into the faces of all these academic enigmas, I wondered again what I was doing there. I felt like a fish that had happened upon a shark's meeting and only failed to be noticed due to its inconsequentiality; I felt like a fraud. So, it was a relief when I escaped from that first meeting unscathed by any requirement to participate but intuiting that I was swimming waters far deeper than I knew. It was no surprise when, barely out the door, I caught myself trying to make an excuse to skip the next meeting.

My saving grace was I had experience in persevering alone in foreign places. I knew how to nod my head in a parody of wisdom and to avoid saying "Wee" at all costs. I could manage my fear of (figuratively) getting kicked to the floor or slapped if I said something wrong. Most importantly, I knew to keep my mouth shut as I dug in to listen, and listen, and listen, in hopes of learning what I sensed these people had to impart.

In the ensuing weeks, I was surprised by something that should not have been surprising. Despite the treatment staff's academic accomplishments and worldly successes, each of them, except the elder statesmen, Doctors Klement and Schulz, was rendered human by the need to vie for position in the intellectual pecking order.

The psychiatrists had cherished egos and would posture intellectually, theorizing ad nauseum, which would conflict with the nursing staff who faced the practical day-to-day reality of contending with twenty ever-demanding and sometimes combative patients. The nursing staff was not seeking theoretical discussion but concrete directions. Despite the ensuing vitriol, I would learn that these moments of intra-team hostility fit within a broader tapestry of deep relationships and caring that only accrues among those who have been in battle together. In the months and years to come, I would learn that we were all in the trenches, and no one escaped unbloodied, including me.

Within several months, my frustration was profound. All the treatment team seemed to do was talk, emphasizing contemplating thoughts, feelings, and underlying motivations rather than doing anything. The inaction drove me crazy. I wondered, *How are we helping?* I was forever teetering on the cusp of leaving but couldn't. My curiosity would not let me; I sensed that these people held a secret knowledge of life, a mystery, and I wanted it for myself.

I started going to the medical library every free moment, reading psychoanalytic texts over lunch, in my office, between meetings, and at home. For the next five years, I immersed myself in the psychoanalytic literature, paying particular attention to writings on primitive mental states. What I read was often so erudite that it left me cold. Still, along the way, like sluicing for gold, I would unexpectedly come across a nugget of knowledge that shined a light of understanding on what previously had been in shadow, not only about my patients but about me. So, I would haunt the passageways in the library, looking for knowledge in the deeper recesses of the shelves, but with every answer, I found more questions, and with more knowledge came much sorrow.

What I came to understand is that primitive mental states are part of healthy development. Indeed, they are childhood ways of feeling, thinking, and relating that comprise the inner rings of the tree trunk of the psyche through which all of us travel on the road toward psychological maturity. The two-year-old's obstinacy or dramatic loss of control exhibited in an adult is only one of countless examples. As such, primitive mental states are not crazy in and of themselves. Indeed, all people move up and down the developmental scales on a near-daily basis. The difference is that the psychologically vulnerable regress more often and more profoundly or even dwell in these early ways of perceiving and relating.

I also learned that people do not regress haphazardly but to former states of mental/emotional functioning that date to the time when their problems began sending their development awry. Being able to understand and personally relate to the ways of perceiving and relating of my patients helped immeasurably in helping them to understand themselves. I did not look down at them or up at them but over at them. I knew something of thinking in all-or-nothing ways, of perceiving the world and the people who inhabited it as dangerous, of erroneously equating feelings as facts, and of feeling so flooded by emotions that my capacity to think was overwhelmed. I grew to appreciate the central importance of establishing a relationship with the patient, wherein the implicit and explicit, conscious and unconscious communications that are a part of every relationship can help promote human connection and stimulate development.

I imagine some of you taking issue, saying, "I don't regress. I don't enter primitive mental states." But I would respectfully say, "Toro Caca." Have you ever been reactive? Have you never yelled out of control at your kids, spouse, brother, or sister? Have you never experienced the breakup of a relationship or the loss of a loved one like a blow to the stomach that left you wanting to die? Have you never peeked at a Jerry Springer show or been to the dark places inside yourself? Have you never shouted at or imagined inflicting terrible things on the turtle-speed drivers who insist on staying in the passing lane or fail to use their turn signals?

That is what I am talking about, reactivity, without hesitation, self-observation, or reflection. These are the hallmarks of a primitive mental state. Now, imagine not being able to get out of that mental state. Bingo, you are there.

Psychoanalytic thinking helped me make sense of things, not only of *what* people were doing but *why* they were doing it, and to inter-relate how we treat ourselves with how we treat others. I had lived in such states more times than I care to remember, and they return with all their gothic intensity during times of severed relationship or family difficulty.

I had not understood that my learning had started the day I had driven onto the grounds of Sheppard-Pratt Hospital. It had begun as I drank in the sight of the spacious green lawns dotted with majestic trees and the well-spaced groupings of Adirondack chairs. It had continued in the large airy rooms full of light and color, nestled in the protective battlements of those aging buildings. It provided an environment in which it was safe to consider one's thoughts and feel one's feelings no matter how dark or socially unacceptable they might be in the world beyond its borders. Sheppard-Pratt had been whispering its secrets all along; I just had not had the ears to listen.

I came to experience the incalculable importance of having someone to talk to who is honestly interested and thoughtful. Someone not frightened or appalled by the muddy side of human experience but willing and able to explore those dark corners with you. You know you are not alone when you can do that with someone. You come to appreciate that you're not even all that unusual.

CHAPTER 20

Psycho-Analysis

Aside from my wish as a therapist to experience therapy from the inside out, I was in touch with a disquiet I could no longer deny and one I had felt most of my life but always explained away: *That's the way it is. It is just the way I am. It is just the way things are.* But now, immersed in examining the issues of others, I was forever in a hall of mirrors, reminding me of my own and feeling increasingly disingenuous, encouraging others to confront their unrest while ignoring mine.

Unable to afford traditional psychoanalysis, I became a training case at the Baltimore Washington Center for Psychoanalysis and Psychotherapy. I attended four sessions weekly, lying supine on an analytic couch while the analyst sat behind me, out of sight but certainly not out of mind. I had no real goals other than to go through the experience so I could see what it was like and, perhaps, deepen my understanding of myself. Still, trepidation lingered. A friend had entered analysis several months earlier and told me how, after just a few short minutes lying on the couch, his feelings became so intense that he shot bolt upright and could not continue.

Just think about that. You are lying on a couch talking with someone sitting behind you, and the experience becomes so overwhelming that you feel compelled to sit up as if you just stuck your toe in an electric socket. Is it possible that confronting the workings of one's mind is one of the most courageous things a person can do?

Now, it was *me* in that circumstance, lying on the analytic couch, my horizons limited to the ceiling of the room and the wall beyond my outstretched feet. The analyst sat behind me. The object of our mutual attention? *Me.* The only instruction was, "Say whatever comes to mind without editing." From the outset, it was disconcerting. There was no other guidance, no questions asked to direct me, and no indication of what topics I should discuss. Out of my field of vision, I could not read the analyst's facial expressions or body language. Even garnering cues about what he might be thinking or feeling from his speech was nearly impossible, given he was a man of few words. Even when he did speak, it was not in a conversational way but as pointed questions, observations, or commentary, too advanced for my consideration. In a typical session, he might not say more than twenty words. I found all of this increasingly annoying. After all, *If I knew what to think, why would I need him?*

Left to my own devices, feeling the need to fill the vacuum of silence, I soon became a blathering idiot. What could I possibly talk about for four hours a week with a person I couldn't see and rarely responded? I didn't have much to say, or at least not much I thought was worth saying (I was immediately editing). I was rapidly discovering that it was relatively easy to be in the role of a psychotherapist, listening as the patient supplied the grist for the mill of therapy. It was quite another level of difficulty being the patient, expected to provide that grist.

Such a lack of structure fosters regression, and in psychoanalysis, that is the intention, taking the patient back in time to childhood ways of perceiving and relating. My thinking soon blurred as I wrestled with my thoughts, particularly as my internal board of critics devalued almost anything I might consider saying. My mind shied away from saying anything that would leave me open to possible censure, either in the form of the therapist's private thoughts about me or my scathing self-criticalness honed at the feet of my father. Add to this caustic soup the sarcastic and competitive quips of my brothers echoing unbidden in the corridors of my psyche, and the situation became a cocktail for mental paralysis. I could now understand why my friend bolted upright after just a few minutes on this rack of self-recriminations.

Assured of the vapidness of my thoughts, I experimented with different subjects, trying to discern which, if any, would elicit a word from my therapist, which I interpreted as having earned his interest and hopefully elevated me in his eyes. Such an outcome would keep me momentarily safe from the shame or ridicule I feared.

My mental gymnastics exhausted me, for no matter how hard I tried, I could not stop relating to my invisible therapist as if he were a stand-in version of my father or siblings. I attempted to take control of the situation by trying to provoke a response from my therapist, sometimes saying the most inappropriate things that came to mind. My initial pristine goal of self-understanding had quickly become secondary to my need to trigger a reaction from my therapist around which I could organize myself and fashion a response. So deep was my need for some connection, any connection, even if it was a connection to a stand-in for my noxious father. What did I get back? Typically, silence.

Absent the external cues to which we all usually moor ourselves in human interactions, I slipped anchor and was adrift in the swirling currents and eddies of my mind. I wished for something around which to center my world, something not unlike the back of that chair in the dining hall of Collège St. Etienne. The security strategies devised subconsciously in the formative years of my development had organized my understanding of life and relationships and, most importantly, how to keep safe, strained to wrap themselves around this formless experience.

The smoke and mirrors of my imaginings became a wormhole catapulting me back in time to primitive childhood ways of thinking and feeling. I discovered what people learn in a sensory deprivation tank: there is no place in this world or beyond more frightening than our minds. Or, to paraphrase Freud, "There is nothing so frightening as the return of the repressed."

Worn down by the constant, paranoid, urgent nudging of my psyche, I realized that I needed to find a way out of this labyrinth of self-criticism and the fear of rejection or attack that formed its walls. Therefore, I did the one thing still under my control: I quit. I gave up the futile effort of worrying about what my analyst might be thinking. Instead, I chose to focus on *my* thoughts and feelings, finally adhering to the impossibly simple yet incredibly difficult analytic injunction to "Say whatever comes to mind without judgment or censorship." I had stopped projecting my internal negative self-talk onto my therapist and let go of focusing on the critical voices in my head, recognizing them as the root of my self-inflicted misery, and the first impediment to my recovery and growth. In this way, I finally settled into treatment. The process of psychoanalysis had amplified my disquiets, not relieved them, and thus gave them a voice. No longer nameless, I could now think about them.

I soon discovered that the most productive sessions occurred when I relaxed into my stream of consciousness. More substantive thoughts and feelings had space for emerging in these relatively calm and more transparent waters of my psyche. These denizens of the deep would rise slowly to the surface like manatees and become illuminated in the moonbeams of my awareness or by the analyst's comments, facilitating further discoveries.

I had entered psychoanalysis determined to endure the experience—to see where it and I would go. As deeply disturbing as it was, the process was not as bad as I had feared. After all, my bar for isolation, loneliness, and being left with only my thoughts and feelings for company was high. Even so, inexplicably, I did begin crying that first session and every session after that for the next six months. Only later did I realize that the isolation of psychoanalysis, my seeming inability to connect with my therapist, strummed the taught chords of the terrible emptiness of my childhood. It was all there, and it was happening all over again in the *right now* of my regression.

What I learned in four years of psychoanalysis can be summed up in a few words. But do not misunderstand; psychoanalysis was not a waste of time, far from it. It was life-changing, fostering emotional development, not merely intellectual insight. This growth required the entire four years lying supine on that couch that became home as I time-traveled through my life.

I will spare you slogging through all the psychological swamp mud with which I dealt and, instead, jump right over to the firm ground of what I learned. First, having recognized the failed strategy of trying to be dependent upon my analyst, I turned to self-observation and reflection to assess what was and was not important in my life.

With this painfully won shift in focus, I settled into treatment, studying my thoughts, feelings, and sensations: the mental contents of my psyche. In doing so, I came to appreciate my analyst as someone upon whom I could rely to insert himself into my musings when he felt he had something to offer. His role was not to lead the way but to follow alongside as a faithful companion, lending the staff of his powers of observation and thinking to supplement my own. Unattached to me and not having lived my upbringing, he could better see with fresh eyes and identify the unseen waters of my life. He assisted in my evolving from a self-suppressive tyrannical psyche to one of greater psychic freedom, valuing freedom of thought and speech above all else—that liberating process took a year.

That may sound like a long time, but it is a mere fleeting of the wind if you consider its nature. I was on what the psychoanalyst Melanie Klein called *the road toward autonomy*. The word "toward" is used because one never fully arrives.

In the second year, I learned the importance of confronting my fears instead of running away. When I faced my fears, I could begin to think about them. They became manageable and often dissipated altogether. It was a lesson I had learned before: something seemingly unmanageable from a distance can be overcome, often easily, up close, a step at a time. I learned first-hand what the famous psychoanalyst Winnicott was referring to when he noted that fantasy without the limiting effects of external reality is like a locomotive without brakes. Thus, an internal play space gradually unfolded in which I could consider my thoughts and feelings from different angles because I no longer feared becoming them.

I discovered that psychotherapy is a revolutionary process, helping me break free of the constraining rings of my childhood and its legacy of self-fettering prejudices and assumptions. Ironically, these convictions I had learned from the *adults* in my life who *did* tell me what to think and feel in childhood and would do so in my adulthood if I let them. I further recognized that my parents, as well as the generations that had preceded them, had imbibed the imparted *truths* of their elders with hardly a hiccup, their ways of being and behaving passing down through the generations without a second thought or even a first.

I finally understood that to the degree any of us goes unthinkingly along with the familiar and the familial, we are living cookie-cutter lives, just marching in lockstep with earlier generations, only singing new renditions of the same old songs. In my case, this included the ingrained belief that quitting is always wrong, that one should endure without complaint and be gallant (whatever that meant), and that I should stay on the periphery and support others but not expect success, much less demand it of myself.

In the vernacular of the army brat, I exclaimed, "I want to become the top master sergeant at Sheppard-Pratt Hospital." In the medical model, psychiatrists, followed by psychologists, were the officer class, while the best a social worker could hope for was to rise to the top of the non-commissioned ranks. I aspired to become the Senior Social Worker of Adult Long-Term Inpatient Services. This position entailed supervising social work services on seven inpatient units covering 140 patients with diagnoses ranging from personality disorder to eating disorder to schizophrenia.

After a short silence, my analyst, himself a psychiatrist, responded with a deceptively simple and softly posed question. Those five words he spoke that day, like a tiny pebble thrown into a pond, would create a ripple in my psyche, a turbulence towards a world of unimagined potential that would forever change my life. "Why just a master sergeant?"

PART IV

THE WORLD AND I—CO-MINGLING

Now I was breaking out of my shell into a world I was helping create. Instead of feeling like a leaf swept along in the river of life, I was actively swimming and choosing my direction. The possibilities were many: I could swim against the current or with it, or I could swim to the shore and hike cross-country. Nothing was fated; I was shaping my world as the world was shaping me. Now, we—the world and I—were co-mingling rather than co-mangling, engaged in an inter-enriching relationship. I could live with that. Hell, I could thrive.

CHAPTER 21

"Why Just a Master Sergeant?"

Why just a master sergeant?

Those words hung in the air and then careened around my brain like ping-pong balls in a lottery machine. Numerous glib responses sprang to mind, but I could not push the question away.

It was not only the question but the fact that he, a psychiatrist, had asked it. *He could imagine my being more than a master sergeant, so why couldn't I?* I could not imagine how rising higher in the professional ranks was an option, but he could. My analyst had given me a gift: an unfolding horizon rife with the possibility of potential yet to be birthed.

In the prototypic framework of my familial role, I was always the support person or spectator, while Jacques was center stage. To me, taking the spotlight had never been a consideration: it just was *not* the way of things. In the following months, I recognized that I had patterned my existence on this habituated role and its implicit, unconscious assumption, even going as far as recreating my familial role as a support person within the treatment team. There, the psychiatrists stood center stage, and I played the part of the younger brother.

But what was my alternative? How could I compare to people from Vienna, Harvard, and Yale and all the medical and doctoral programs the others had attended? How could I overcome the *medical model* of the hospital where psychiatrists ruled and social workers were lower on the caste system? In this model, my role fit me like an old suit; it felt like a part of *me*.

As I considered the question, "Why just a master sergeant?" I realized I couldn't wholly attribute my life as a spectator to the familial and familiar. I reasoned that to sustain such behavior, I must find it rewarding in some way. I soon realized the reward was a protective one. Being center stage would make me vulnerable to attack, criticism, second-guessing, and getting knocked down.

Conversely, if I kept a low profile, my chances of remaining unscathed would be better unless, of course, I counted the cost of a self-limited life. If I wanted to see who I could become, I would have to put myself out there. The difference was that I was no longer a defenseless boy. I was a grown man who could stand up for himself.

Beleaguered by such thoughts, I groaned as another consideration took hold. Surprisingly, I was worried about Jacques. I knew, even if he did not, that he was as dependent on his role as I had been on mine. If I changed my role, how would that affect his?

Indeed, these were childish thoughts—the thinking derived from childhood typically is—but that did not make them less potent, but more so, connected as they were to the powerful feelings of that more emotionally charged and splintered age. It took a while, but I worked it out. If I were to take responsibility for *my* happiness and meaning, I would have to continue evolving. If Jacques came to feel threatened by my growth, which I very much doubted, then he would have to do more maturing as well—there is nothing wrong with that.

With those concerns laid to rest, the final layer of my resistance came fully to mind with nauseating intensity: what if I failed? The limelight would offer no place to hide. The shame, humiliation, and damage to my sense of self would be devastating. Didn't it make more sense for me not to try and, thus, never fail?

In the end, these concerns gave way to a certain knowledge: I would be tormented for the rest of my life, forever disappointed in myself, and always wondering who I might have become if I did not try. I could not bear the idea of the road not traveled, of not exploring where it might have taken me. My choice stood between the risks of moving forward, possibly into a spring-fed life, or dwelling in a growing pool of resignation and stagnation that would eventually hook up with its compatriot, despair, as my yesterdays became my tomorrows till the day I died. Then the question, "What's the point?" would become trenchant. So it was that while I was teetering on this edge of indecision, a fundamental truth dawned upon me with startling clarity: the pursuit of happiness and meaning, at least for me, required the courage to put myself totally on the line and the courage to fail.

I began speaking up in team meetings. Using the mindset developed in psychoanalysis, I focused on expressing my thoughts as they pertained to the clinical cases rather than concerning myself with what others might be thinking about me. I discovered that what I offered was usually taken seriously. One team member remarked, "Charlie, you're making people think." And then, some months later, something unprecedented happened: Dr. Klement invited me to the weekly meetings for psychotherapists.

The wonderfully freeing thing was that although I did not know where any of this would lead, I had come to appreciate that that did not matter. What was incredibly valuable was the palpable experience of being more fully engaged in my life. At that time, however, I did not yet understand that this more fully invested life would lead to other experiences and events that I could not have imagined, and not a few of which I wish I had never come to know. Nevertheless, despite the times to come that would sometimes brim with anguish rather than joy, I am far better for it.

CHAPTER 22

Anguish and Joy

Psychoanalytically oriented psychotherapy challenges me to the core, not just the ongoing training and education. The therapist must also attend to his mental and emotional workings, assessing the silent, subconscious communication between patient and therapist.

Self-examination is not always pleasant. It is disquieting to confront one's vulnerabilities—the dark feelings, hypocrisies, and lies that we are all prone to tell ourselves. Nonetheless, a willingness to do so is necessary as part of the implicit contract for any therapist who opts to work in an insight-oriented way.

This challenge can be formidable when treating people suffering from significant psychopathology, especially borderline, narcissistic, and paranoid personality disorders. These individuals, gifted in their ability to read the dark undercurrents in others while denying similar feelings within themselves, often lack empathy. As a result, they are prone to launching ruthless attacks on the self of anyone who displeases them.

Working on B-2 was already challenging. On any given day, I could find myself physically restraining a patient as she bolted from my office in a bid to escape, confronting a patient holding a shard of a broken lightbulb against her throat, threatening to cut her carotid artery if I did not unlock the door; or, striving to remain calm during a man's agitated rantings while silently praying he did not attack.

Nonetheless, as dramatic as these occurrences were, the worst challenges were in the patient's attack on the therapist's self, accusing them of being sadistic, lustful, greedy, hateful, envious, or jealous. Or to be taunted and called "small-dicked" or "lower than whale shit at the bottom of the ocean." What makes these imputations so unsettling is that if honest with oneself, there is often a smattering of truth. Every human being has within them measures of these elements—lust, flaws, weaknesses, and feelings of shame and inadequacy. When such aspects of the human condition are focused on and amplified under the microscopic intensity of the patient's laser vision while simultaneously being evoked and provoked by the patient's behaviors, these flaws are magnified, seemingly more significant than the whole. They threaten the capacity for sober reasoning and the ability to retain the light of day.

There is an old proverb: sticks and stones may break my bones, but words will never harm me. If only that were true, but we are more than bones. Words can damage your spirit, heart, and mind, for they never arrive alone. It is how they are delivered, be it with contempt, scorn, or disdain, alongside the provocative behaviors designed to elicit the very feelings of which I am charged. One patient keeps bumping into me as we walk down the hall while accusing me of not liking her. Another contemptuously mocks me for lusting after her while crossing and uncrossing her legs, flashing her underwear, and leaning forward so that her blouse falls open, exposing her breasts. A recently discharged patient assured me he has a gun and taunted me: "Don't you believe me? Do you want me to show it to you? Are you afraid? Are you a coward?"

Such a barrage of personal challenges endured week in and week out forged a mélange of fact and fantasy, fueling self-questioning and self-doubt, threatening to wrest my sense of reality. You see, I was annoyed with the girl who kept bumping into me as we walked down the hall. Did that mean I did not like her? I was titillated by the woman who repeatedly flashed me. Did that mean I lusted after her? I felt frightened by the guy that threatened me with the idea of a gun. Did that make me a coward?

Yet, as personally challenging as these interactions were, the most unsettling experiences occurred when an entire family chorus such sentiments. On one occasion, a delusionally paranoid family, rife with fears of persecution, would accuse me of saying things I did not think I had said. When I attempted to explore their assertions, they would claim to quote me from a discussion that had occurred minutes earlier, challenging my capacity to recall specifics under the emotionally charged, mind-fogging barrage of their accusations. Often, they would change one or two keywords, use words out of context, or actively interpret what I did say in persecutory ways. Under the pressure of this inquisitional force, it became problematic for me to keep an open mind and maintain perspective while constantly being put on the defensive and trying to sort out what was real and what was delusional.

For example, when I was taking the family history, the father pugnaciously announced, "I didn't grieve the death of my mother. I was glad she was gone." Later, referring to this comment, I said, "You were glad your mom was dead." As if poked with a hot iron, the father took furious exception to my words, spitting out, "I didn't say that! Those aren't my words! You are putting words in my mouth!" The sons and daughters-in-law added their chorus of outrage, the abrupt intensity nearly sweeping me away. All the while, the mother sat silently, her worried eyes flicking here and there like a terrified mouse trying to find a hiding hole. I now knew the feeling.

Overwhelmed by this unexpected upsurge of vehement protest, I struggled to recover the father's exact wording, all the while fearing, given the absolute certainty of their convictions, that I had invented my interpretation of the whole exchange. Fortunately, I was able to recall his words. "I believe you said, 'I was glad she was gone.' I'm sorry if I misinterpreted this to mean you were glad she was dead. Tell me, how should I have understood it?" At this, the father paused, face rigid, and entered a brooding reproachful silence as if he recognized the meaning of his words for the first time and that my intent all along had been to stab him with them.

I was the outsider and, from the beginning, the enemy. My every attempt to engage with this family only spurred their sense of endangerment, as if I were trying to invade rather than to relate.

This family drama was one of many reality-undermining interactions with some patients' families. With them, I always strove to remain open to the family's perceptions, working hard to create a culture in which all things could be considered, including the limitations of the therapist. While an important goal, this striving required I tolerate uncertainty, a state of mind I call "Not-Knowing," necessary for examining things from all perspectives. Conversely, the families, ensconced in the protective battlements of absolutist, all-or-nothing thinking and feeling and armored in the unquestioning certainty of their beliefs, were free to spout their righteous indignation. Thus, mine was the fate of a flickering flame in a tornado.

What was real? What was not? Repeatedly caught in such Byzantine considerations, I would feel a growing dread in anticipation of meeting with these families and knew that this would not do. I fell upon a common-sense solution. I needed someone in the room that was not caught up in the emotional fray. I needed an objective observer who, free from the need to interact, could more easily maintain perspective. I invited again invited the mental health worker, Rob, to join me in the sessions. Slight of build, solicitous and ebullient, Rob was well-liked by patients and staff. I told him his job was to listen so that, when needed, I could ask, "Did I say that?" or "Did I misrepresent that?" What amazed me was that the families readily accepted what Rob said, his role as The Observer seemingly lending him credibility. Thus freed, we moved forward in the family work.

Within the first few months of joining B-2, the treating psychologist and I decided that a home visit for a patient, Joan, was necessitated. On Friday, Joan reported a phone call from her aged mother, who was said to be in poor health and was rapidly deteriorating: Joan exclaimed that she needed to visit her mother before it was too late. The next team meeting wasn't until Monday, and time felt to be of the essence. Neither Joan, the psychologist, nor I thought we could wait. In addition, the psychologist and I were frustrated with the passivity of the treatment team and took this opportunity to act on our own. That is how I came to be driving Joan to see her mother.

On the way, an alarming indicator that this decision was not well thought out arose when I asked myself, *What will I do if Joan tries to open the door and jump out? How would I stop her when I'm driving?* Fortunately, nothing happened, and we arrived at her mother's senior high-rise apartment without incident.

As I sat quietly to the side in the well-ordered living room, listening with half an ear as Joan spoke with her mother, I noticed additional hints that this plan had been ill-thought. I felt played and strangely betrayed. I hadn't thought that, given our connection, Joan could have done this to me. Joan's mother did not appear near death's door or anywhere in its vicinity. She was well-dressed and groomed, and there were no nurses or medical devices in view. Perhaps the only thing I found at odds was her determination to be grim and embittered by our presence. Sharp as a tack and just as biting, she showed no affection, recoiling from Joan's every attempt at connection like a queen from the repulsive touch of a lice-ridden beggar. After a quarter-hour of this thorny reception, Joan, a look of resignation painting her face, announced she had to go to the bathroom. I was uncomfortable letting her out of my sight but had no choice. I certainly could not follow her to the bathroom.

While Joan was in the bathroom, I tried to strike up a conversation with her mother. Then I tried to figure out how to end it when she remained aloof and as engaging as a mannequin. Now, I just wanted to escape and began wondering what was taking Joan so long. As the seconds trickled by, my concern rose. I asked Joan's mother, "Do you think she's okay?" Smiling the smile of someone who had just bitten into a lime, her eyes suggesting some secret knowledge I did not possess, the mother dismissively waved aside any need to worry. That is when a thought slammed into my mind—*She wants Joan dead. Joan is going to be a good daughter and comply.* I sprang to my feet and hurried to the bathroom door.

I knocked gently, calling Joan's name. There was no response. I hoped she had not heard me, then prayed that her silence was due to embarrassment over doing her business with me just outside the door. I called again, this time louder, and still, there was no answer. Alarm growing, I called out a third time, only to be met with that intractable silence, stoking the flames of my concern into a bonfire of fear.

At just this moment, Joan hesitantly responded, "Just a minute." Something wet and ugly twisted in my belly. *Why had Joan failed to respond for so long? Why was her speech hesitant?* All these questions pointed to one answer, an answer that I did not want to believe: I was running out of time. I commanded, "Joan, open the door right now!" Silence.

I turned the knob, but the door was locked. Terrified but fully committed, I backed up and ran at the door, ramming it with my shoulder, splintering the lock. The door swung open. Inside, Joan stood two feet away, bent over the sink, focused entirely on her wrist, razor blade poised.

Shouting, "No!" I lunged. I don't know how it happened; perhaps it was the rush of adrenalin or a heightened sense of things, but in that moment of insanity, everything slowed. I took in the razor, slowly cleaving its way across Joan's wrist, flesh unzipping and yawning open in a scarlet scream. Frightened, angry, panicked, and betrayed, I grabbed the hand holding the blade and banged it against the sink, shouting, "Drop the razor! Drop the razor!" until she did. Freed from that threat, I clutched her injured arm above the gash, fighting to stem the flow of blood while wrestling her to the floor, yelling sharply to her bitch of a mother, "Call 911. Do it now!"

The EMTs arrived minutes later to find me on the floor, holding Joan in place as I clutched her injured wrist, stemming the flow of blood. I followed the ambulance to the emergency room, knowing two things with certainty: "I'll be fired," and "I should be." Joan suffered a partly severed tendon. Fortunately, she later regained the entire functioning of her hand.

The following Monday, *I* was the focus of the team meeting, at the center stage that had been so elusive. Only instead of being lit with grandeur, I burned with shame, my humiliation laid bare for all to see. The team reviewed the entire episode step by agonizing step. As staff members asked their questions, some took extra care to add a reprimand. I sat and listened, saying not a word in defense. I had no defense; I was guilty.

All the while, Dr. Klement listened, exhibiting her enduring quest for understanding. She seemed aware that I was unforgiving of me and resigned to my fate. Near the end of the meeting, her cultured Austrian accent and bearing lending its usual thoughtful formality, she softly spoke, "Charles, perhaps in the future, you should reconsider when you feel the urge to operate outside the auspices of the treatment team." Nothing more was ever said.

With those words, Dr. Klement informed me that I still had a future on B-2. As you can imagine, there were no shouts of joy or patting of shoulders. However, I am forever grateful. While I was castigating myself, Dr. Klement had been integrating the conflicting aspects of the situation. I *had* made a serious error in judgment, but it was not malicious. I was also genuinely remorseful. She knew me to be an earnest person and refused to allow this singular, if epic, mistake to define me. Thus, she helped forge me into a humbler, wiser, more compassionate version of myself.

CHAPTER 23

"Follow Me and Become as Lost as I Am."

Roger Lewin, MD

The value of the experience I am about to share is that it stripped me of many conceits I had as a therapist and reminded me that I am simply a fellow traveler in this unpredictable and uncontrollable journey called life. When reduced to my essence, all I have to offer is integrity, an analytic mind, and a genuine desire to understand other people. For the most part, this has been good enough.

I once read that the words love, care, and cure share the same Latin root. I have cause to doubt the veracity of this, but I like the idea. Caring for someone is an essential part of the therapist's ability to be of help. Though not sufficient unto itself, care is necessary, conveying love and acceptance, two experiences of which the patient is usually bereft. The presence or absence of care, even if never spoken, is felt in the care--filled interactions of psychotherapy.

Given that the therapist/patient relationship is the bedrock of the treatment effort, losing a patient to suicide is extraordinarily disturbing, especially when you had no inkling it was coming. I am left wondering, *Why did she do it? Why didn't he talk to me about it? What was going through her mind? Why didn't I see it coming? How could I have prevented it? How could I have missed it?* With the absolute finality of suicide, such questions can never be answered because death cuts off all inquiry: I can never ask her, and she can never tell.

Of course, part of the responsibility belongs to the patient, but part belongs to me. The blame, if one is inclined to blame, can never be apportioned—this much hers, this much mine—because we never fully know why something happens. The possibility that I might have done something different, something better, something more, or something less, is forever present and can never be entirely laid to rest.

Eve, a small angular woman in her late forties with short-cropped black hair matted to her crown, was married and the mother of two teenage boys. She had an extensive history of psychiatric hospitalizations, suicidal behaviors, and physically and emotionally abusive treatment of her husband and children. But what made Eve stand out was the degree to which she somaticized her feelings, her unexpressed feelings becoming inscribed in the body. It was rumored among hospital staff that due to her vociferous complaints of physical pain over the years, every organ that could be removed from her body had been, yet no physical problems were found.

The early weeks and months of the family sessions were leaden affairs. Eve held center stage while George, her husband, sat stiff-backed, dressed in his ever-present suit, and related monosyllabically. The two boys sat silently, sullen, as teenagers the world over are wont to do. Yet, they seemed to drink everything in with their big eyes. I treated the family on B-2 for six months and then on an outpatient basis for another year. During this time, Eve's ability to express her feelings grew, along with her relationship with her husband and kids. Progress had been on a long upward trend. Issues were discussed, family relationships had become more secure and relaxed, and everyone was happier.

I was beginning a one-week vacation, cooking steaks on the grill for family and friends on a sunny, humid Saturday afternoon, the sound of water splashing and kids' laughter floating over from the swimming pool. The phone rang. It was George, "I'm sorry to disturb you at home and on your vacation, but I have nowhere else to turn." Dread filled my chest, not from any premonition, but because I imagined losing part of this day to work. I asked, "What is it?" Without preamble, George stammered, "Eve shot herself in the head. The ambulance took her to shock trauma.

There is blood all over. I cannot handle it. The kids are at the beach, due back this evening. I don't want them to see it. I have no one to help me. Will you help me?"

I struggled to take in what George was saying. It stood in such a dark and ugly juxtaposition to the sounds of life and laughter surrounding me. I heard his words, but it was as if they came from a different universe. They did not fit this beautiful day or what I thought I knew. I had no concerns about Eve killing herself. Indeed, I had been happy with the way things had been going. But then, his words and their meaning sank home: What I thought I knew and what I knew were two vastly different things. *How am I to come to terms with that knowledge?*

I immediately became self-preserving. I did not want to help George; I especially did not want to rip myself away from this beautiful day to enter the carnage of his life. But it was already too late. Looking at the steaks on the grill, picturing the aftermath of Eve's shooting, I had the moronic thought: *Steaks will never look the same again.* With the pull of a trigger several miles away, my day had just been obliterated. I overrode my self-protective urges, recognizing that I could not leave this man alone in the wreckage of his life or allow his kids to return from a day at the beach to a home turned killing ground. With trepidation, I bid farewell to the party and drove the lifetime away to Eve's house.

George stood on the concrete stoop of his rowhouse, overlooking a barren postage-stamp yard, with his usual reserved demeanor; the tremble of his chin and his shaking hands the only indications that he was barely holding together. As I approached, he flatly announced, "Eve has been declared dead."

Walking towards him, I noticed dark spots on the crumbling sidewalk, my mind reeling from the omen they portended. I followed George and the trail of drops inside the house, where they staggered up the worn wooden steps to a second-floor bedroom. There, a blood-spattered wall and ceiling, and a small lake of drying scarlet, mottled with liver-colored chunks of brain, told more than one would ever wish to hear as they spoke the unspeakable. I fought the urge to gag while suffering a child-like fear that whatever calamity had befallen Eve would snake out from under the bed and grab me by the ankle. I wanted to run. But I had to help George and protect the kids from these appalling images that, if seen, would haunt them for the rest of their lives.

George and I gathered mops and rags and began the gruesome task. Laboring in a trance-like state, passing sluggishly from one erratic thought to another, I recognized that I had agreed to join George in this ghastly world in part as an act of penance. Having misread the situation, I had been unable to prevent it. Indeed, I had not even seen it coming. *Did George hold me responsible? Perhaps his call for help was an expression of his anger, forcing me to face the terrible consequences of my failure,* although nothing of the sort was said. I did not think to ask why he had not called a professional crew or made up a reason to tell his kids not to come home. My thinking had been simple, *He called. I must answer. It's not only about cleaning up; it's about being with someone, about not being alone.* Moving from one splash of gore to the next, trapped in a bloody world without horizon, I could not finish a thought and did not want to feel a thing.

As I scrubbed the ceiling, rubber-gloved hands covered with gore, drops of liquid fell onto my upturned face. Recoiling from its touch, filled with unease, I hurried to wash. Returning to my work, I rinsed the washcloth in the bucket, dumbly noting the water turning pink.

It was surreal: sweeping Eve's brains into a dustpan and putting them in the trash, the work gory, and the symbolism horrid. I numbly moved from the bedroom ceiling to wall, to floor, to stairway, to wooden steps, and out onto the sidewalk. I made repeated trips to the tiny kitchen through the cramped dining room for clean water, sometimes exiting to the backyard for a breath of fresh air. All the while, I imagined Eve in each place where she had ruled and lived and the family life that had unfolded within these dreary confines.

I had met with Eve three days earlier, and everything seemed fine. She had been relaxed and happy, and I had thought we were all enjoying the benefits of our work. Over the months, we struggled, suffered, and laughed together. Now, incredibly, without transition, we had all been wrenched into another reality, terrible in its finality and indelibly stained with shock and horror. I questioned everything I thought I knew: how could the world have changed so drastically without warning?

This new world in which Eve, a living, vibrant human being, had been reduced to bits of brain matter and puddles of blood, being tossed out like the trash and, sadly, unimaginably, that I, her therapist, was the one doing the tossing was incomprehensible.

I had given up smoking, but now, the need gnawed at me from within my chest like a rat trying to free itself from a cardboard box. I took a Salem from a pack Eve had left on the kitchen counter, and lit it up, all the while wondering, *How can I stand here and smoke one of Eve's cigarettes, in a sense, breathe in her air while she lays dead?* Crazily, I felt both intrusive and impolite, but my urgent hunger to satisfy the scratching of that nicotine fix was irresistible.

George joined me and haltingly said, "Eve left a suicide note, telling me she loved the boys and me. She valued the better relationships that everyone was feeling. Still, inside, she was experiencing a growing urge to harm again and becoming ever more fearful of losing the gains she had made. She said she could not put the kids or me through that again. She would not allow that to happen." Emotions began constricting George's voice, and he paused to collect himself. I sat silent, unable to think of a thing to say. I tried to absorb what George was telling me, what Eve had been feeling, but it was too much to take in. George continued: "She had laid my best suit out, and next to it, a dress she wanted to be buried in; both had been dry cleaned. Her note was pinned to my suitcoat along with cash she had saved to help pay for the funeral. She said she didn't want her death to be any more of a burden than it had to be."

While George spoke, his words started to register; tears welled in my eyes and then coursed down my face: Eve's terror had been of herself; her suicide was an attempt to protect those she loved.

It was evident that Eve had been planning her suicide for some time, suggesting that her more recent emotional stability and contentment had not only risen from treatment efforts but from the relief she had gained from deciding to take control of her life by ending it. Of course, I will never really know. All I know is that I regret Eve did not share her concerns with me and that we never had the opportunity to see if we could have made it through the labyrinth together. Of course, for Eve to have been so transparent, she would have had to risk the possibility that I might have taken control of her via hospitalization.

I left George that night in the care of a neighbor, but I could not leave the memories behind. Emotionally battered and besieged by images that would crop up throughout the day and night: the chunks of brain matter, the blush-colored water turning scarlet, and the tactile memory of the blood-tainted drops falling onto my face all burned their way into my psyche. Sitting with friends in a restaurant, I would suddenly associate the food with Eve's brain matter or a ruby-colored glass of wine with her blood. A word spoken in conversation would prompt an association to something she had said, hurtling me back in time, lost to the moment. While my friends chatted in companionable relationships, I would linger in an alternate universe of blood and despair. I was not remembering; I was reliving: the past became my present.

I did not reveal my troubled state. What would be the point—to destroy the mood of my companions? So, I remained alone with it, and it remained alone with me, re-emerging episodically and unpredictably for several years until it finally faded away, like the color going out of an aging photo. Now, I can remember without reliving that day, at least most of the time.

Of course, I questioned myself, *What could I have done?* However, I could not think of anything. Eve's presentation had been seamless, her suicide entirely unexpected, a humbling and troubling reminder that I may not know what I think I know and that none of us ever fully knows the mind of another.

Eve had been living in fear of herself. I cannot imagine living a life fearing your reactivity, not knowing what you will do next, not knowing whether you will hurt your sons, stab them in their sleep, or whether your spouse, tired of disappointments, will up and go or not. Faced with such dilemmas, I understand why she chose to take her life. Some might say, "She didn't have to; she could have had help if only she had let me in on her fears," but I find that a bit presumptuous. In truth, there are no guarantees we would have succeeded; maybe Eve knew she did not have the emotional resources to face the challenges ahead, or perhaps I wouldn't have been up to the task.

These are sobering thoughts, but I would not have it any other way. The ego-humbling experience of knowing I know far less than I like to think leaves me feeling more securely rooted in the terra firma of reality rather than in the crumbling sandcastle of ego and personal myth. That gravestone marker in Tombstone, AZ, has wisdom: "Be who you is, cuz if you be what you ain't, then you ain't what you is."

CHAPTER 24

The Goths Are at The Gates

By the mid-1980s, after the kids were in school, I felt Jane should return to work. I did not grasp the level of her discontent with this change. She wanted to be a full-time homemaker and was surprised by my insistence, thinking we were happy. Indeed, mostly we were, but I was increasingly feeling displaced by her child-centric focus, her catering to each kid's every want and the financial pressures of being the only bread earner. I did not see having a part-time job and taking care of the kids as mutually exclusive, mainly when the kids were in school. I was wrong. Believing that Jane's return to work meant she had accepted my position, I did not realize that inwardly, she simmered with resentment. Though words were spoken, I was deaf to their meaning.

As if my professional life felt like it needed to correspond to my personal life, things started to shift there as well. Corporations around this time began hiring companies to lower healthcare costs. Shamelessly, these companies referred to themselves as *Managed Care* companies, as if *caring* had anything to do with what they did. In truth, their only concern was to amass more profit by lowering costs by eliminating care, and they did so without mercy or morality.

Their strategy? The managed care automatons put providers under siege through near-daily audits of each patient's medical records and ceaseless demands for phone interviews in which they plumbed for any reason to have the patient discharged. These agents of managed care companies made life-changing determinations without meeting the patient. They claimed to ascertain all they needed from reading the medical record and questioning staff on the phone like attorneys taking depositions. I can only conclude that it is easier to risk the destruction of someone's life when there is not a face attached to it.

In short order, the staff started trying to protect the patient by *proving* the need for treatment instead of focusing on the treatment itself. The expression "*Treating the medical record*" was born.

But that was not the end of it. The outrageously evil thing was that when these managed care companies succeeded in driving the patient from inpatient care, having touted the viability of outpatient options, they would question the patient's need for outpatient treatment.

The utterly absurd aspect of all this is that outpatient sessions were approved like a miser's doling out of pennies: on a once-a-week basis for four weeks at a time, at which point, treatment would be terminated, or the entire charade repeated.

Time, space, and safety are necessary to heal the human psyche. However, these companies managed to undermine any notion of sanctuary or asylum, inpatient or out. This was true even when four weeks of sessions were repeatedly authorized. Why? Because the imminent possibility of treatment cancellation hung heavy in the air, destroying any hope of the patient or therapist being able to relax into treatment; no therapist wants to open a can of worms that they might not be around to help the patient resolve. To paraphrase Winnicott, "You can't practice therapy in a burning building."

And if a patient committed suicide, like Pontius Pilate washing his hands, the managed care acolytes would say, "That kind of thing happens. After all, they are psychiatric patients."

I hated the disingenuous bastards. One reviewer insisted that I allow a patient to take a day pass with his family. When the patient returned unharmed after having spent the day surrounded by family, the reviewer declared this as *proof* that hospitalization was no longer required. When I asked the reviewer with genuine curiosity, "Off the record, as a clinician, are you okay with this? Does this make any sense to you?"

She stammered, “That’s not the point. I’m merely following the rules here.”

When I countered, “That sounds dangerously close to Nazi prison guards saying they were only following orders,” she hung up the phone. This exchange earned me a rebuke from the office of the hospital's president; the managed care company had complained. I asked, “What did I get wrong?”

He responded, “Comparing her to a Nazi. She was distraught.”

I said, “Again, what part did I get wrong?”

Exasperated, he shouted, “She was upset!” as if her upset was a clinching argument.

I answered, “Good. She should be. Maybe I helped her out.”

One day, as the treatment team was again discussing discharging yet another patient due to managed care pressure, I could contain myself no longer. Filled with outrage, I burst out of my chair, shouting, “This is bullshit!” and stormed out of the room.

At this point, recognizing my reactivity and the uncontainable nature of my feelings, I had to wonder, *What’s going on with me?*

I plunged into the shame and fury I felt when my dad slapped me around or demeaned me and the incalculable rage at his ordering me to keep my hands clasped behind my back, thus making me party to my victimization while he freely slapped my face.

I remembered how my fear of confronting the wrong of racism had turned me into a coward in that Montgomery, Alabama, movie theater and how I had been intimidated by the MPs and not returned to assist the mixed-race couple in the car in Heidelberg.

Now, I was being pressed into destroying something I loved: a place where wounded souls might rest and recover, the core need of which I fully understood. That was unbearable; I had found my voice and the wherewithal to do something in the face of wrongdoing, even if the only thing I could do was to name it for what it was and call it out as both ignorant and morally bankrupt.

What got to me when I descended from my moral high horse is that such horrid behavior says something about us human beings. We all wax eloquently about the wrongs done by others, such as the horrors imposed by Hitler in the concentration camps, Pol Pot in the killing fields of Cambodia, or Donald Trump's inhumane separation of children from their parents. And these people do not act alone. What about all the people who support and carry out such policies?

The point is that none of us is immune from greed, envy, or doing what we're told, even if it's wrong. All that is part of the human condition, but the least we can do is struggle with those decisions and acknowledge our guilt. Integrity is essential in the journey toward a happy and meaningful life. A positive sense of self depends more on doing the right thing than personal aggrandizement or material gain. And the ones to be afraid of? Those who claim to do no wrong.

Reluctantly, I began accepting that the era of long-term inpatient care was over and started writing. Career ambition wasn't the motivating force. Indeed, given the primal intensity of my feelings, ambition was nowhere to be found. Instead, I felt a compelling need to get *something out*. At the start, I did not know what that something was; I had no words for it. But, like a glowing ember, it burst into flame as I began to write, and the words came rushing in.

What emerged was an attempt to articulate the lessons learned on B-2. I wanted to preserve an understanding of the vital necessity of sanctuary and asylum and how to implement it on an outpatient basis in individual and couples therapy. Of course, psychoanalytic theory had always addressed the importance of asylum, but I needed to add my voice. While writing, I became aware that writing was my way of grieving, coming to terms with the destruction of B-2, the equivalent of a Stradivarius violin, being dismantled piece by piece and turned into a child's toy by arrogant vandals.

It took me a year to author that paper, which underlined the importance of creating a treatment space where each spouse could think, feel, and voice their more intimate thoughts and feelings without fear of shame, blame, attack, or demand for change. Titled, *The Borderline/Schizoid Marriage: The Holding Environment as an Essential*

Treatment Construct, the paper was published in the *Journal of Marriage and Family Therapy (1989).*

It was around this time, following Jane's help editing this paper, that the first crack in our relationship started to show. That paper had stimulated unpleasant memories of her childhood; for the first time, she revealed she had had a history of self-cutting.

But, in truth, the seeds of the demise of our relationship were there from the beginning. Unconsciously, I had chosen someone who was the opposite of my father did who did not threaten me with domination. In doing so, I chose someone who had difficulty asserting her own needs and would come to feel dominated by me. Where I did not want to be subjugated, Jane perceived me as conquering. Where I thought conflict did not exist in any meaningful way, it was there aplenty, just kept quiet in the tribunal of Jane's mind. There, I was accused and found guilty. Unaware of these proceedings because of Jane's difficulty in asserting herself, I could not plead my case; I did not know there was a case to plead. Accordingly, over the years, I was convicted of crime after crime in the sealed courtroom of Jane's mind, assuming the characteristics of her critical and rejecting mother and the hated attributes of my father.

But even if we had been able to talk about it, I doubt that much would have changed: we were too different, each moving in a direction not to the other's liking. Jane had passively gone along with most of my wishes, such as the trip to Mexico and Baltimore. She also supported my working and going to school full-time, even though this shifted the burden of childcare to her. She had yet to find her voice, at least one strong enough for me to hear.

Reciprocally, I met her need to have someone lead the way who could maintain the illusion of knowing what he was doing. I was the verbal and outgoing one at parties; she was shy and uncomfortable. She was the one who wanted to leave early, while I wanted to stay late. Over time, I felt burdened by her insistent need to go and embarrassed by her passivity. I found her falling asleep in the coat room when we did not leave humiliating, as she must have felt equally controlled by my desire to stay. We began taking two cars. It seemed like a brilliant solution; I did not appreciate the symbolism at the time. Even if I had, I doubt I would have changed it. And thus, we went, each in our direction, so slowly that it was not apparent but as steady rain, ever leaching nutrients from the soil of our relationship.

Where our needs had meshed in our early years, our needs of the middle years pushed us apart. Jane expressed hers in the uncomplicated metaphor of wanting a small brick home with a white fence and more children, her version of the TV series *Little House on the Prairie*. Jane had a real and vital need for a quiet, uncomplicated life. She wanted a sanctuary and an asylum, a safe space in which she could emerge in her soft-spoken way to be herself. My need was more aggressive; to explore new worlds and to expand my bounds.

I kept thinking we would adjust to one another, that we could bridge the divide. I kept telling myself, "All we need to do is hang in. We will find a way." But even with couple's therapy, that was not to be: our needs were in fatal antagonism with one another.

CHAPTER 25

Coming Home, Again

Ring. Ring. Ring.

My sleep-addled brain struggles to wrap itself around the sound until I realize it is the phone. In the dark, I grope and bobble the handset to my ear, croaking out, "Hello."

A man's voice answers into my mouth: I was speaking to the receiver. As I struggle to fumble the phone around, his words keep sliding off my ears. But eventually, after this inauspicious beginning, I piece together that the man is Bob Winer, a psychoanalyst affiliated with a training program in Washington, D.C. He says, "We would like you to present your paper at our annual conference."

My paper? What paper?

As if reading my mind, he explains that Patricia Alfin, one of my supervisees, had sent a copy of my paper to the Washington School of Psychiatry; she had never mentioned this to me. Then, like the facets of a Rubik's cube falling into place, I understand, "*Jesus, this is The Washington School of Psychiatry. They want me to present my paper on treating the borderline/schizoid marriage at their annual conference.*"

The Washington School of Psychiatry is one of the country's premier schools of psychoanalytically informed psychotherapy. I had taken a workshop there years earlier and had been highly impressed. Flattered, I responded, "Sure, be glad to," trying too late for an air of nonchalance.

It was 1990, and these were heady times; I was not accustomed to recognition. Occasionally, feeling full of myself, I would allow displays of conceit to seep out. Thus far, my major accomplishment was becoming the Senior Social Worker of Adult Long-Term Inpatient Services at Sheppard-Pratt in 1988.

As I began to appreciate the depth of the leap I was making, a panic gradually took hold. When Bob invited me to read my paper, it sounded straightforward: I'd read it. *How hard could that be?* But now, having learned that I would have thirty minutes to present my paper, followed by a question-and-answer period, it had assumed daunting proportions. The audience would include over four hundred psychoanalysts, psychiatrists, psychologists, and social workers, from around the world. I would be asked unscripted questions from a knowledgeable audience, many trained at Harvard, Yale, Oxford, London's Tavistock Clinic, and the University of Edinburgh, all far better educated than me. I also learned that what I had written fell into a theoretical orientation called the Psychoanalytic Object Relations Theory of the British School. That was a mouthful; I had no idea I had become a part of it. Unlike me, most attendees had heard of the British School of Object Relations, and many had written books and papers on the subject.

Primarily self-taught, I felt utterly outclassed. Finally, there was my lack of public speaking experience: only one sparsely attended talk at Sheppard-Pratt, which I nervously read, sounding like a chipmunk on steroids. With the conference looming, the real possibility of public embarrassment took hold, and sleep became ever more elusive.

On the first morning of the four-day conference, I met Dr. Winer and Drs. David and Jill Scharff. Each of the first two had degrees from both Harvard and Yale, and Jill had graduated from the University of Aberdeen, Scotland. The Scharffs had trained at the world-famous Tavistock clinic in London and were the director and co-director of the school. Each had written a handful of books on psychoanalytic theory and practice. I was a dwarf among giants.

That morning, I would co-lead a small group of attendees with David Scharff. The group's purpose was to help the participants process the day's presentations. Having little group experience, no formal education in object relations couples and family theory, and no experience in training others, I had little to offer.

That afternoon, my discomfort grew as I co-led a group with Jill Scharff—now realizing they were evaluating me. Though I would later come to know Jill as a caring and supportive person, on this day, she was aggressive with both the group and me: in front of the group, she criticized me for being too passive. I felt like a man without clothes. That evening, I left the conference feeling fraudulent for being there as a faculty member and worried about what was to come.

The following morning, in the faculty meeting, the small group leaders unanimously reported that the attendees were dissatisfied with the conference, finding it neither illuminating nor engaging. At the end of their reporting, David Scharff solemnly asserted, "It's up to the presenters this morning to save the conference." My spine turned to goo. By my accounting, there were only two speakers that morning: Jill and *me*. Dismayed, I replayed the words "save the conference" in my head and wondered, *Who are they kidding? I have already demonstrated the vast limits of my knowledge.* I imagined the upcoming debacle, and fought to calm myself, reasoning that Dr. Scharff could not be talking to me; he must be talking to Jill. She was the one that was internationally recognized and respected; I had one small journal article, eleven pages, to my name. I looked over at Jill, who appeared calm and completely unruffled, exuding steadfast confidence. Buoyed by her authority, I happily imagined myself being pulled along in the wake of her stellar presentation.

After the faculty meeting, battling an anxiety that threatened to overwhelm me, I could not sit still. Accordingly, I elected to observe Jill's presentation from the empty balcony, where I would be free to exit to the upstairs hallway without disturbing the proceedings and pace to my heart's content when I felt the need. That was a good decision. I alternated between listening to Jill's presentation and pacing the outer hallway. Gradually, my jitters bled off, and I became more confident that I could get through this with a modicum of self-respect left intact.

That is until I returned from a trip to the hallway mid-way through Jill's talk, just in time to capture an acerbic interchange between her and the audience. I watched the fractious interaction in wide-eyed horror, having no idea what had happened. Later, I learned that Jill had chided the audience to "put down your pens and listen." My anxiety soared like a kite whose string had been cut. I thought, *Oh my god! I will be such a lightning rod for all the ill-contained furor of the audience. They will pick me apart as an embodiment of the inadequacies of the conference.*

I spent the next few minutes before I was due to speak, pondering on the best exit strategy. There were only two appealing options: run for it or pretend to lose consciousness. Considering the audience, the second plan had obvious flaws. I still do not understand what forced my feet down the stairs and across the stage to join the faculty. As I took a chair, a fellow faculty member leaned over and whispered, "I thought you had run for it." Having my assessment of the situation so concisely confirmed, including that the thought of fleeing was not beyond the pale, made me laugh. Looking into the eyes of the academic elite, their faces already set in a grimace of disappointment, I again wondered if I could still make a run for it. Perhaps feign a short call only never to be seen again? The room was filled with animosity; it wasn't just a conjuring of my anxiety-ridden mind. Deep into my musings, I barely heard when someone began calling my name.

After months, the moment I had anticipated with dread and excitement was upon me. It felt surreal. I felt strangely removed, unknowingly dissociating from the calamity that was close at hand. I rose on wet-noodle legs and wobbled up the stairs to the stage, my head feeling like a bowling ball stuck on a stick of over-ripe celery.

There, I confronted a mind-boggling apparatus: the podium. I stared at it incredulously, not having a clue as to what to do. It was a technological marvel worthy of the Starship Enterprise. There were buttons for lights and volume dials, pin microphones for lapels, standard microphones attached to the podium, handheld microphones for walking around, and dimmer switches to adjust the lights for reading. There were also buttons for slides and videos and for moving the entire apparatus up and down, and buttons and switches whose functions I couldn't begin to fathom.

That is when I made my first mistake. I looked up and into the unblinking eyes of the tripod-mounted cameras dotting the auditorium, their muzzles sighting in on me, ready to capture my every utterance for posterity. Then I took in the audience and realized it had grown quiet: They were waiting for *me* as I just stood there, feeling inanely proud that I could stand at all.

Finally, an assistant, recognizing my bewilderment, joined me on the stage. Mics went on my lapel, microphones adjusted, the podium raised, and the lights amplified. He also poured me a glass of water from a pitcher atop the podium, a kindness I was absurdly grateful for, given my trembling hands. If left to myself, I imagined spilling water over the rostrum, shorting out the whole apparatus and, thereby, the entire conference. Dumbly, I thought, *Wouldn't that be a moment in the sun?*

At this time, I slowly became aware that the audience had grown eerily silent, holding their collective breath as they sensed the precariousness of my mental state. The hum of social noise was now wholly absent; I was unmistakably the sole focus of all four hundred and twenty sets of piercing eyes and unsmiling faces. I looked out at them as they looked in at me.

Realizing that my mouth was chalk dry and that I needed a sip of water before speaking, I slowly extended my trembling hand towards the glass situated at the far reaches of the podium, my arm feeling robotic and no longer a part of me. My hand reached the glass an eternity later. Breathing a sigh of relief, I prayed that I would not knock the glass over while instructing my fingers, one by one, to wrap themselves around it. This feat accomplished, I thought *I'm halfway there. Don't hurry. Take your time. Grip the glass but not so hard as to break it.*

When my hand completed its trembling return voyage from the podium to my mouth, the water was sloshing, threatening to spill over the sides of the cup. But this was not the worst of it. I could not have imagined the worst of it. When I put the shaking glass to my mouth, it ticked against my teeth, and the microphones were only too eager to pick up the sound. "Tick, tick, tick," "Tick, tick, tick," the rapping of the glass against my teeth faithfully amplified throughout the auditorium for all to hear; "Tick, tick, tick."

Horrified, I had an out-of-body experience of watching the entire auditorium, including myself, from on high. That is when I noticed that I had unwittingly accomplished the most amazing thing: I had rendered an audience of over four hundred people silent and mesmerized. It was entirely still, not a movement, a cough, a sniffle, or clearing a throat. Entranced by what they sensed was the beginning of a ten-car pileup of a presentation, the audience, like rubberneckers the world over, could not tear their eyes away.

After tick, tick, ticking myself through several sips of water, I managed to affect the lumbering return journey of the glass to the podium. Then, I could delay no longer: *No climbing back down the ladder,* and, thinking, *fuck it,* I leaped. I began speaking, but instead of seeking the illusion of safety in the written word and launching like that Chipmunk of old into reading my paper as fast as possible to get the whole thing over with, I felt a need to stave off the unbearable isolation I felt. I spoke extemporaneously, referring to the crosscurrents of tensions rippling through the auditorium that morning and to my manifest anxiety. My first words were, "I guess this is what's called a pisser."

It took a moment for my words to register—such vocabulary is not a standard part of highbrow conferences. Scattered laughter broke out, slowly gaining momentum as more people realized what I had said. I said, "For some reason, the words 'I guess we're not in Kansas anymore, Toto' keep running through my mind." The audience at large broke out into laughter. It was a warm laugh. It was not at me, but with me, both heartfelt and welcoming. The audience could identify with what I was going through, and I could relate to the anger in the room.

After waiting for the laughter to subside, I read in a conversational tone. I had written the paper with this aim in mind, with a reminder to speak slowly written in the margins. I also interrupted my reading several times to look out at the sea of faces and ask, "Are you with me?" I wanted to maintain that connection and invite questions if there was any confusion. The response was a resounding "Yes." When I finished reading, the audience began applauding, the sound gaining as it went, forming a series of sonic waves that washed over me again and again. It was glorious. The applause went on and on and became the closest thing to a standing ovation in a professional setting I would ever receive.

The tension-filled context in which the audience and I found ourselves paved the way. I had not talked down to them or up to them. I had shown human vulnerability without pretense or apology and soldiered on giving a good paper and an accessible story.

After my talk, I went to the restroom. A guy came up to the adjacent urinal, began his business, then looked over at me, saying, "Man, that was great. Really good job." Throughout the day, others offered similar praise. Treated like a celebrity, I tried to contain how puffed up I felt. And then, as the day wore on, I reached my social threshold. My face hurt from smiling, and my brain hurt from the effort of making small talk: I just wanted to go home.

Following that talk, the leaders of the Washington School of Psychiatry invited me to join the faculty. Not wanting to drive to D.C. from Baltimore for the many meetings it would require, and given that my family was beginning to fall apart, I opted to become Guest Faculty. In the years to follow, I grew to love these people who were so unstinting in their willingness to share their time and expertise. They did not do this for money; there was no money. They did it for the love of their profession and analytically informed psychotherapy.

Later, Bob Winer and his wife, Bo, would welcome me into their home and provide support during one of the most trying times of my life that was beginning to break upon me in full force like that tsunami of old.

PART V

SWALLOW THE SHADOW

It was here that monster that had been chasing me all my life. Except now I understood that it had not been chasing me at all: I had been carrying it the whole time.

CHAPTER 26

Love Stories

As a couple's therapist, I enjoy talking about relationships; that is, everyone's but my own. Not only are my relationships personal and sometimes embarrassing, but I also cannot hide the identity of the people involved. Even so, I must talk about what I can.

I have been addicted to love. I have found and lost several loves. I learned how a relationship could seem to change suddenly when the seeds of its demise had been there all along. I have discovered how needs change over time and that what attracts in one era can deter or even repel in another. I have learned how you can be with someone for years and never really know them and how time or events can flip a switch and change people in unanticipated ways.

I must also confess a problem with listening. Most of us do not listen well, and I can be as guilty as the next, hearing what I want to hear and minimizing or misinterpreting the rest. Like most people, I pay selective attention and have a restrictive memory that tends to support my view of myself and the world around me.

Yet, despite these impediments, I have learned from my relationships. Remarkably, what I have learned always boils down to the same lesson, just given in different ways. The teaching is akin to a multi-faceted diamond spotlighted on the black velvet of a slowly turning pedestal. I stare at a facet of the problem, then just when I think *I've got it*, the pedestal turns, revealing the same problem from a different perspective. What's uncanny is that each lesson always points back to me: I am responsible, and my happiness is up to me. I now understand that when I hold others accountable, I, not they, are guilty of wrongdoing.

Accepting responsibility for one's happiness lessens the burden we place on others. The result is that when two relatively independent people get together, they do so because they *want* to, not because they *need* to.

I understand that my over-romanticized notion of love, the blinding kind so eulogized in movies and songs, is not loving at all. When *blinded by love,* I impose my internally fabricated fantasy of the Other upon the other. How can that be *love*? Of course, my mental creation of the Other *is* incredibly enticing. Why wouldn't it be? Created by me, my Other is forged by my deepest needs and can easily fulfill them with one caveat, "If only She would."

When my construction of the Other is burning hot, the experience intoxicates with promise. Of course, if my needs are frustrated, *She must* also be the cause: rejecting rather than nurturing. Thus, my *Imaginary Other* shape-changes between a woman who excites my every yearning to a woman who holds my needs in contempt and delights in frustrating them. All the while, needing to preserve my idealized image of her, I secretly feel I deserve it.

Jane and I journeyed together for twenty years; the early ones were relatively happy. We had made our trip around the country, returned to school, and weathered the car accident. However, things went bad, really bad. Unbeknownst to me, Jane's discontent, forever feeding upon itself, only festered. One evening, as I tried to talk through the unhappiness between us, Jane burst out of her shell, vehemently reciting a catalog of my complaints from a piece of paper. This inventory included every critique I had ever made during our twenty-year relationship. Recited all together and all at once, they formed a punch to my heart that woke me to her primal, red-eyed rage.

I was utterly taken aback. I had not known Jane had been listening, much less taking my criticisms like stabs to the heart. But there they were, like bodies frozen in a cryogenic tank only to be brought back to life en masse, imbued with a zombie-like horror. In Jane's mind, I was selfish, self-absorbed, self-centered, over-controlling, attacking, belittling, and incessantly pushing her to live *my* way. I could not imagine a more damning portrayal, encompassing every personality trait I hated in my father and leaving me feeling ugly and repellent.

I erroneously believed that I had separated from my father after confronting him on two occasions, both in my early thirties. In the first, I had risen from the dinner table to get seconds when he barked at me in a condescending voice, "Charlie! Bring me more roast beef!" In our earlier years, he had often referred to us disparagingly as his "little n**gers." Now, his tone triggered those deep-seated feelings of humiliation within me. Also, talking to me in this debasing way in front of my kids was intolerable. I would not stand for that.

While a primordial fear grazed my spine, the hollow echoes of painful memories of abuse under his quick, eager hands, I sharply responded, "No! I'll bring you more roast beef when you ask politely." Silence filled the gulf following my rebuke. As would any narcissist, Dad refused to apologize or ask politely. And like any narcissist, he never got up to get the roast beef.

The second instance occurred when the family gathered around the dinner table in animated conversation. I had begun to insert myself into the flow when Dad, sitting catty-corner to me, without warning, slapped me sharply on the forehead. I instantly recognized that he felt stymied, given his difficulty getting a word in and that I had been the handiest outlet for his frustration. But I would not be his whipping boy anymore. I immediately struck him back on his forehead with equal force, and in a low, tight voice, my eyes fixed like a bayonet upon his, said: "Dad, don't *ever* hit me again."

He looked straight at me, then for a weapon, his eyes falling upon his steak knife. He looked from the blade to me, then back to the knife, and started moving his hand. With genuine disdain, words dripping with the acid of my contempt, I challenged him: "Really? You're going to kill me?" After a long pause of consideration, the tension left his body. He never hit me again.

These events signaled my willingness to end my relationship with my father and, if necessary, with my mother. I *wanted* my parents in my life, but not at all costs.

I did not recognize that putting Dad in his place in the physical world had not gotten rid of his ubiquitous presence in my internal one. I could swallow but not digest.

And so, Jane tried, and I tried, but in hindsight, there was never a possible repair. When relationships become so de-illusioned, there never is. In the meantime, Jane was in torment, unable to recapture her love for me, leading her to question her capacity for love. All this was made worse by her remorseless self-damnation: her mother's voice calling from the grave.

Caught in an unrelenting web of conflicting desires and strictures, Jane tried all means to escape her self-loathing and communicate her rage to me in non-verbal ways. She binge drank and went for long runs only to be brought home by strangers upon whose yards she had passed out. She agreed to go into therapy. But then, her psychiatrist called: she had arrived intoxicated with our kids in tow.

Jane tried gaining control through bouts of anorexia with purging and by soothing herself through delicate self-cutting so extensive that the brown scabs appeared to form leather bands on her arms. Then the suicide attempts began, gestures really, but ones that could have easily led to her demise: overdoses of prescribed medications combined with alcohol. Numerous intensive care visits and psychiatric hospitalizations followed.

I was reminded of Eve, my patient who committed suicide. Once again, I felt fooled—all this time, I had thought things were going okay, only to be reminded that you never really know what goes on inside someone's mind. Only this time, I was not the therapist, trying to help her from a more distant position. This time I was George, the husband. Would I be the one coming home one day to find Jane dead from an overdose? Would I be the one to remove her body before the kids would see it, cleaning up the blood?

Constantly tormented, I worried about Jane, the kids, and myself. The kids called me daily at work, anxiously noting bloodstains on the cuffs of Jane's blouse or her carrying a brown paper bag they feared contained alcohol into the house.

For a long while, my primary feeling had been empathy for Jane, alongside fear and helplessness. But after several years, I was worn down and grew angry as Jane continued her slide, subjecting the kids and me to terrible fear and anxiety. Finally, I drew a line, telling Jane that I would support her going to the hospital but would leave her if she continued to seek hospitalization via self-destructive acts.

All the while, as frightening and dangerous as these years were, a part of me admired Jane. I recognized she was running with the wolves and fighting an epic battle. I did not know if she would win or what shape winning would take. From meager and abusive beginnings, Jane, now in early middle age, was fighting to claim her life and find that voice she had been missing. She was breaking out of her timidity and the shadow of her mother, which now overshadowed me. This life-giving need was so compelling that it erupted with the ferocity of someone clawing her way from the cold depths of a mountain lake to the sun-lit surface for air.

There is nothing more heartbreaking than to ever so slowly, over months and years, come to understand that you are toxic to a person for whom you care. It is a slow roast over an open fire, skin bubbling as you rotate on the turning spit. Through Jane's behavior, she communicated her feelings in the most direct and over-powering ways. As a result, she became increasingly more toxic to the kids and me.

Jane continued suicide acting out. She later told me, "Once you drew a line, I felt compelled to cross it" Enough was enough. I met Jane in the psych ward and told her I was separating. We wept together, the rending one of the most painful experiences in each of our lives that had already known their measure of pain. So many years traveled together, and now our time was ending—something neither of us had anticipated or would have scripted.

I grieved for Jane, the children we loved, and all the things we would no longer share: Christmas mornings, Thanksgiving dinners, watching our children grow up in the same house, and growing old in each other's company. Instead, a future that had once seemed well-established now lay wide open, a vast, flat, wind-swept tundra on a grey winter's day. Its frigid barrenness stretched farther than my heart could bear.

In this way, I became a single parent, staggering under the loss of my wife, the challenge of trying to run a household and meet my kids' needs, themselves angry and heartbroken. Add the absence of family support in the area, the financial pressures of maintaining a home on a social worker's pay, and the cost of various therapies for family members, including inpatient hospitalizations for Jane, and you begin to appreciate the spirit-sapping pressure I felt. Depression, anxiety, and exhaustion became my companions, and suicide a considered option: I lost forty pounds.

Having always fended for myself, I often did not realize when I needed help. Reality broke through the walls of my ignorance, for no matter how hard I tried, I could not find a way to be in different places simultaneously. I marveled at how people I barely knew were ready to help, often offering what I had not recognized I needed: help with the kids, a place for them to stay after school, and the occasional cooked meal, to name a few. It was humbling and heartwarming, reminding me that I was not wholly alone unless I made myself so.

All the while, I was treating patients and going about my business as if everything were fine– aside from crying between appointments. To my surprise, I found myself more, rather than less, emotionally attuned to my patients; my empathy and my work were deepening. As my patients were struggling with their impossible situations, I was struggling with mine. My treatment skills were developing. I could hear more, listen better, and relate more fully. Just like Jane was discovering new dimensions of herself, I, too, was uncovering new dimensions of mine.

CHAPTER 27

Meeting Myself

How? That question transported me to the time of my separation from Jane when I had lost forty pounds without trying and just wanted to stay in bed. Ron-Z suggested we go rock climbing at Wolf's Head in the Catoctin Mountain Park, near Camp David. Lethargy lay heavy upon me, but I knew I had to do something. "A day in nature," says Ron, "just the thing."

It was a warm, humid, sun-soaked day. The hike was laborious; up and down hills and through the forest until the cliff rose before us like the curved bow of a ship. Fifty yards wide and thirty feet high, rounded boulders littered its base impersonating ocean waves. The western part of the cliff fell off gradually, but the eastern one was a sharp vertical.

Ron and I clambered up the western side, taking in the arboreal view of the valley below and the range of luminescent blue hills cascading to the horizon. What had seemed a steep climb from afar, swallowed whole by the eye, was easily managed up close when taken step by step. Consequently, this tame experience did nothing to get me out of my hopeless thoughts and depression. I gradually shifted east along the base of the cliff, trying more challenging climbs. Then, skin glistening with sweat, I stood at the Wolf's Head: the true vertical.

I thought, "I think I can do it," and must have spoken aloud, for Ron asked, "Are you sure?"

I smiled, thinking that most things weren't certain anymore, "I have no idea, but it will be interesting to try." Thankfully, the fog of my depression was already lifting as I considered the challenge. *Thirty feet is not all that high, and if I can clear the first ten, I can make the rest. The only problem is the boulder-strewn ground at the base of the cliff; there is no safe place to fall.* Ron opted to walk around and meet me at the top. Standing at the foot of that sheer height, I remembered that traveler of old who stood at the brink of a yellow wood. And just like that traveler, I was faced with two roads: I could walk around or climb the cliff. I had always wondered what sight that traveler held at the end of his journey. Perhaps, I would soon find out.

I began climbing, quickly entering a rhythm, reminding myself to maintain at least three points of contact while moving the fourth limb, arm, or leg, to the next point of purchase. Plastered against the cliff wall, cheek to mottled stone, my perspective reduced to the grain of the rock in front of my eyes, I would tilt my head upward to look for signs of another quarter-inch fissure to hook with my fingers. I would grope blindly below with my foot for any outcropping upon which to wedge the sole of my boot, first one, then another, and on I went.

A moment arrived when the next handhold was not readily apparent. I used this break to take in my surroundings: *Oh shit. I'm twenty feet up!* After pausing for breath, I resumed my search for another handhold only to discover that the rock was smooth. What had begun as a trivial concern grew more acute as the cliff face refused to give up its secrets.

I considered climbing down but ruled that out, imagining that lowering myself up and down with one leg to feel around with the other blindly would soon drain the support leg of strength. Heart sinking, I re-examined the cliff face, soon acknowledging that desperately wishing for something does not make it appear. With mounting apprehension, I readjusted the parameters of my search, now looking for any blemish on the rock's skin. I finally saw a shadow that might or might not be a small outcropping. The bad news was that this imperfection, now a mark of beauty, was four inches beyond the reach of my outstretched hand.

I must jump for it. It was a shocking revelation, an insane idea. My imagination proved to be quite astute in such times. *It could be a ledge, but maybe it is only a shadow. If it is a ledge, it might be too narrow or covered with sand-like pebbles that could cause my fingers to slip.* It was a small leap, barely more than a stretching of the toes, but the consequences were devastating. Serious injury, if not death, was in the offing. Fear constricted my chest, making breathing harder, and my legs began to tremble with the strain of clinging to the cliff's face—I feared cramps would soon follow. Another unpleasant fact dawned upon me: I could not keep this position forever and certainly not long enough for help to arrive.

At this point, Ron, curious about the silence, peered over the cliff's edge ten feet above, anxiously calling out, "Charlie, are you alright?" Given the precariousness of my situation and the worrying I was in the midst of, that question struck me as oddly hilarious. A full-body laugh erupted from within me, accompanied by a burst of words I had not known were there, "I think I just met myself!" It was then the revelation struck home that resonated with my situation today. Stripped of all fantasy and denial: I had gotten myself into this situation, and no one else was going to get me out.

My relationship with Jane now felt oddly like my position on the cliff-side: what felt like the safest position, the most familiar, secure, and stable, was the only position that guaranteed I would fall.

Another leg tremor brought me back to the present, warning that not only did I have to leap for that shadow of a ledge, but I had to do it now. Chattering thoughts and fear would only weaken me. With this consideration, I pushed aside doubt and uncertainty as luxuries I could ill afford. In their wake lay the resolute calm of acceptance. I took a deep breath, gathered my strength, readied my legs, then leaped, my fingers scrabbling blindly up the rock wall, clawing their way to the shadow of a ledge and me to my fate. Moments later, I made it to the clifftop. Ron pulled me over, asking quizzically, "What were you laughing about? And what was that about meeting yourself?"

I smiled, answering, "I have no idea." It was all too much for me to process at the time.

Now, all these years later, I realized I was on another cliff, securely ensconced in the familiar self-limiting and self-destructive patterns of my life. I would have to confront that bereft feeling of childhood, the fear of which had hijacked my life, to have any hope of coming out on the other side. I would have to face what I feared most, calling as it did to a time of unremitting loneliness and dread.

Outside of work, and after grocery shopping, cleaning the house, cooking dinner, intervening between bickering children, and nurturing them to the best of my compromised ability, I would retreat to my room and collapse on the bed, alone and forlorn. I walked in a world of broken shadows. The feelings associated with Collège St. Etienne had returned with a vengeance; the nightmare made worse in that my children were sharing in it. As I had lost my mother, they, too, had lost theirs.

On numerous occasions when I ran errands to the grocery store or the mall, I noticed people walking by, excitedly chattering away, seemingly happy and untroubled, which only amplified my feeling of loneliness. I wondered why such devastation permeated my life from my childhood. I recognized I was the only constant in the equation, so I must play a central part in it. I returned to therapy.

I had left psychoanalysis in the middle of my marital troubles because it did not provide the active support and advice I needed. A colleague referred me to Len Press, LCSW-C, whom I had been distantly aware of as a grandfather of clinical social work in the Baltimore area. Therapy with Len was not psychoanalysis but psychoanalytically informed. We sat facing each other, and he was interactive. His constant, compassionate presence helped me contain and make sense of my emotions.

He explained that the loss of Jane reawakened the feeling of abandonment I felt at Collège St. Etienne when I was eleven and twelve. I already knew this, but he expanded my understanding by pointing out that the developmental task of the typical ten to twelve-year-old is to begin separating from home, moving incrementally away from the family towards a peer group and the wider world. For me, there had been no choice. It had not been a self-directed movement, and nothing was incremental. There had been no known culture, language, or peer group to hold me. I had been torn from my family and set adrift in an alien world.

The resulting feeling of abandonment and aloneness took root within me and, to some extent, remains to this day. Bunkered in the ashes of the years gone by, it still bursts into flame given an ill wind. With the loss of Jane, that wind was blowing with tornadic force, returning me to that time of loneliness and despair that felt without end. Thus, as Jane struggled with her demons, I grappled with mine.

Upon discharge from the hospital, Jane lived alone for many months, continuing a course of life-threatening acts and hospitalizations. She only stabilized when I advised my daughter not to attend a discharge planning meeting during her last hospitalization. I had seen my girls assume a parental and caretaking role with Jane, supplanting their own lives. I knew that continuing to participate in discharge planning meetings would only foster that pathologic role reversal. Her failure to appear at this meeting was a wake-up call for Jane: she did not want to lose her daughters. That was Jane's last hospitalization.

Over time, Jane settled into her new life, and after months of stability, I invited her to move back into the house; I would move out. Jane could become a full-time mother again, and the long journey of healing between her and the kids could begin.

Months later, I received a letter from Jane asking for a divorce. In it, she expressed concern I would be angry and feared I would want to hurt her in some unspecified way. That revelation revealed far more about her childhood history than having any relationship to who I was and what I was about. Contrary to her fears, I was not angry; I had gotten by that. Instead, I felt relieved. By initiating the divorce, Jane freed me from the abiding concern that I would be abandoning her if I left. Something I could not do, given my own searing experience with abandonment.

Amazingly, despite the intensity of the marital conflicts, the undercurrent of care we had for one another was always apparent, and the divorce went smoothly. Over the years to follow, Jane attended AA meetings and continued individual therapy. She also took yoga classes and attended a Buddhist ashram.

Jane returned to work, formed many valuable friendships, and devoted herself to the care of her seven grandchildren upon retirement.

Where once she had been absent from her children, she is now fully present and an integral part of their lives. She lives with her husband in a small brick home he grew up in, happier than ever and a living tribute to the power of resiliency and her indomitable spirit.

CHAPTER 28

You Can't Get There From Here

It was 1994, age forty-five when as I sat in my office, the phone rang. The caller introduced herself and then launched into a question that caught me entirely by surprise, so much so that I asked her to repeat it. She said, "Would you be willing to accept nomination as the 1994 Clinician of the Year by the Maryland Society of Clinical Social Workers?"

My first thought was that a friend was putting me on. But, as she continued, I realized she was serious. A relative social isolate and not given to active participation in any organizations outside of the Washington School of Psychiatry, I had no idea what she was saying. Even so, I wondered: *Why would any organization reach out to me, a virtual stranger, to honor me in such a way? It made no sense.*

Nonetheless, seeing no downside, I assured the caller I would accept the nomination. Thinking about the call afterward, I realized I had been a member of the Maryland Society of Clinical Social Workers for years. I hadn't recognized the organization immediately because I had confined my involvement to writing the annual dues check and never attended a meeting.

That week, I mentioned this incident to Len Press. In a curiously guarded fashion, he asked, "You don't know this group?" I told him I had figured that out but that it was hard to imagine them selecting a non-participating member. Len asked, "Do you know when that award began and who the first honoree was?" I assured him I did not know either. He responded, "It began a year ago, and it was me."

Despite vetting the award's validity, I assumed it would be some small, dry, short ceremony and reasoned that I should not take the kids out of school for it. That was until I arrived at the venue and took in the linen-covered tables set for fine dining, formally dressed wait staff, and many people milling about. Introducing myself to the receptionist, I was warmly welcomed and escorted to the head table. I met the honorees for two other awards who had their families with them and instantly regretted not having mine.

As I sat there listening to the other honorees accepting their awards, I thought about what a circuitous journey it had been. I remembered flitting among the shadows in that Alabama woods, my abandonment at Collège St. Etienne, my many failures, acts of delinquency, and nomadic wanderings. I wondered, *What had made that difference in my life?* It wasn't any great intellect or profound wisdom but rather an abiding curiosity and a dogged need to make sense of things. When my turn came to accept my award, I decided to tell a true story that seemed loosely relevant to these thoughts. It did not have a title, but I will give it one now: "You Can't Get There from Here." It speaks to how people can feel lost and disoriented when first setting out on the challenging journey of becoming themselves.

I finished giving Grand Rounds at the Maine Medical Center, Portland, Maine, and a talk at the state hospital and was returning to the airport. As I drove, thinking about the presentations I had given, I became aware of a niggling concern: a lot of time had passed, and I had not seen any signs of the airport. At first, I shrugged off my worry as travel anxiety but as the miles mounted, so did evidence that this was not the case. Finally, I decided to break the cardinal rule of every male: thou shall never ask for directions. The wisdom of this injunction soon became apparent as I got lost further after each stop for assistance. The people were friendly and accommodating, but the multi-step directions and the New England accents made it hard for me to understand what they were saying.

I was now percolating with anxiety as my flight was due to depart in twenty minutes. I did not know how missing a flight would affect me; I had never missed one. My mind cavorted with possibilities: would I be put on standby for later flights? Could I be stranded in Portland overnight? Would I have to pay for a new ticket? Where would I sleep?

Now, with fifteen minutes left until my flight, a last burst of hope bloomed within me. Amidst my cacophony of worries, I saw flags waving in the distance as if beckoning me to a carnival. It was a gas station. I pulled into the station, leaped from the car, and ran into the office. There, I met a dough-faced, stout young man in grease-stained overalls and an orange baseball cap embossed with a truck logo planted crookedly on his head. With arresting intensity, I shouted: "How do I get to the airport from here?"

Interestingly, despite the clamor of my arrival, the young man did not seem to register my presence. Instead, he stood unmoving, glassy-eyed as though in a trance, and so devoid of animation that I wondered if he was aware of me at all. I considered repeating my question but worried that he might be processing and that any interruption could trigger a reboot that could cost valuable time.

Just as I accepted that all was lost, I thought I noticed the slightest movement. *Was desperation prompting me to see things that were not there? Had the young man's eyes exhibited some deep spark of awareness?* I could not tell. Enthralled, I carefully studied him. *Yes! There it was again.* With the ponderous speed of maple syrup on a cold late winter's day, his right hand was starting to move, making its tortoise-like way toward his forehead. Once there, ever so slowly, he pushed his hat back and began rubbing his forehead, effecting a posture that most would associate with ponderous deliberation. As profound meditations tend to do, this process was also taking its fair measure of time, and the last dregs of hope of catching my flight were draining from me.

Then, abruptly, his eyes focused and looked directly into mine. With that, I knew the young man was about to speak. So ready was I for any pearl of information that I felt something akin to what I imagined I would feel sitting at the feet of the Dalai Lama. The gas station attendant, now

Dalai Lama, slowly and emphatically pronounced the following words: "You... can't... get... there... from... here."

Wow! That sentence instantaneously extinguished the last shreds of hope of catching my flight and, with it, all my angst. Just like that, I was no longer in a hurry; there was no place I *had* to be. I now had the unfettered mind, time, and space to consider his words, "You can't get there from here." They were the equivalent of a Zen Buddhist koan or the words of a great philosopher or wise man. I do not think I have ever heard a more Zen-like statement or existential thought. The totality and finality of those words: pure, concrete, absolute, certain, blew my mind. I strived to make sense of them. *What was he saying? What could he possibly mean? Was I in a twilight zone of experience? Were we on another planet devoid of means of transportation? Were we in another dimension of reality where there was no Portland airport?* My mind churned. *How was this possible?*

Although he had unequivocally stated that I could not get *there* from *here*, I was reasonably sure I could. He and I were in competing universes: He could be right, or I could be right, but both of us couldn't be right, could we? I did not want to challenge the young man's assertion and risk giving offense. Indeed, being right was less important to me now than satisfying my curiosity about the meaning of his words. To test them further, I needed to introduce a third possibility, an alternative to the all-or-none option of it being either his way or mine. Looking him squarely in the eye and pointing to the floor three feet to my left, I said, "Okay, I get that. But what if I was standing over there?"

The young man somberly considered my question before snapping his fingers in acknowledgment. Emanating newfound enthusiasm, as if we had just unraveled a mystery of the universe together, he energetically stated, "Oh! You pull right out on the road, take a left, go down one block to the stoplight, take a right, go two blocks till you come to a T at Airport Way, take a left, and it'll take you there."

Hope flared within me, but still cautious, I asked, "And how long might that take?"

"Five minutes."

In the next instant, I was disappearing down the bend, lost in that legendary cloud of dust, and the only sign of my passage was the echo of my shouted: "Thank You!" I made the flight.

That story came to mind because those words, "You can't get there from here," had once applied to my thinking about myself. Nowhere, no how, could I have ever scripted the jumble of paths that took me from that young boy getting his fortune told in those shadowed Alabaman woods some thirty-five years earlier to a man being honored by his peers as a psychotherapist. Nor would I have imagined that much of my success would come from the worse times in my life. Such as my need to convey the lessons learned in inpatient work as it was being suffocated by managed care or my intimate understanding of primitive mental states because of suffering my own at Collège St. Etienne.

What was the key to my transformation? I discovered something both simple and profound. Just like climbing a cliff can appear daunting from a distance but be possible up close, a step at a time, so too life-changing shifts do not have to be epic. They can occur with a slight turn in perspective, achieved with a mere five words, or by moving three feet away.

CHAPTER 29

Post-Divorce

After the divorce, I raced to escape the agony of loneliness and made many of the mistakes people make to fend off feeling their losses. I entered a rebound relationship with Lynn, a much younger, flirtatious, and titillating woman whose smile and light gray eyes sparkled in delight whenever she saw me. I was captivated; for the first time in years, I felt like an elixir rather than a poison. That was heady stuff, particularly when compounded by my readiness to interpret youth for renewal and lust for love. Thus, I became a cliché.

I turned Lynn into my *Healing Amulet* and gave her one to seal the deal. I designed a wedding ring woven with seven strands of gold, each representing a member of the newly formed family: her two kids, my three kids, she, and me. That was my formula: ta-da, instant family.

I would soon realize what I should have known from the beginning. Lynn was not only pretty and vivacious but also unabashedly flirtatious. I had known she had no close female friends but had not fully appreciated that the tributaries to her sense of self flowed from male attention. Although never unfaithful, Lynn was a great fisher of men, continually luring them in and pushing them away in her catch-and-release program. I filed for divorce within three years of first meeting her.

After Lynn, there was another petite, quiet, and sweet woman with doe eyes who also happened to be called Jane. My friends referred to her as Jane-2. Over time, Jane-2's quiet took its customary toll. In response to my growing unhappiness with the absence of connection, she announced that she thought we should live apart but continue the relationship. I had no interest in this but curiously asked, "Would we be monogamous?" Off-handedly, she responded, "I guess so"—that sounded like a "No" to me.

Before we separated, I received an anonymous email accusing Jane 2 of having an affair. I wasn't surprised; Jane had a history of affairs when exiting relationships. She denied the affair in her soft-spoken way, but I had tripped over her lies before when she was embarrassed by the truth. It did not matter. I felt no jealousy. The relationship had been over for some time, even though I, true to form, had refused to accept it.

What surprised me was the depth and breadth of my feelings of eviscerating loss, seemingly entirely out of proportion to the event. Thinking about this over the years led me to believe that not only was I grieving Jane-2 but more so what she represented: my belief in an *Imaginary Other* and the possibility of *Healing Amulets.* For the first time, I acknowledged that the root of my continued unhappiness, both when single and or in a relationship, resided within me and always had: there was no external fix. The broken attachments I suffered during my childhood had become the prototypical structure of my relationships in adulthood. Hope had gone from me.

My belief in the *Imaginary Other* and the possibility of a *Healing Amulet* had provided hope that cushioned the jagged edges of loss and betrayal and the ensuing void that had comprised my early years. My wishful beliefs had somewhat blanketed me from the cold winds of a cratered childhood. But now, I recognized that my fantastical notions of romantic love invariably promised much but delivered little beyond the early spells of symbiotic ecstasy followed by the recurrent bouts of loss and despair.

Now that I had turned to face my demons and the terrible feeling of loneliness from which my fantasies had protected me, I could fully understand why I had needed them. Barely capable of enduring these losses revisited in adulthood, how could the child-me have possibly managed? I would have been completely swept away in the torrent of my despair. My challenge was clear: the problem wasn't other people; it was me. I had to grow up to find a woman I could love securely. I had to evolve the part of me frozen in childhood to learn how to love and be myself in adulthood.

That was easier said than done. I felt utterly orphaned. But I was now willing to pay that price because I understood that if I continued to deny my grief, I would repeatedly re-live it.

In the months to come, I abandoned dating and devoted myself to being alone, committing to that state rather than running from it. Putting to use my capacity for self-observation and reflection, along with the memories of overcoming my fears by facing them, I came to recognize my loneliness not as an enemy but as the old companion it was. I discovered as I passed through the obscuring veils of my fears that I was never alone; for better and worse, I always had *me.*

Recognizing that I was instinctively attracted to women upon whom I could project my *Imaginary Other,* I modified the word radar. I began using the word Gal-dar to describe that acutely attuned, complex, and unconscious system of attraction that went off with all the fanfare of a video arcade machine whenever I was around a woman that would meet my pathologic need. I knew something about this part of the brain: it was in the deepest recesses, before words, and impervious to reason and logic.

What was I to do? How does one talk themselves out of an instinctive attraction? The answer was simple: I did not need to. What I could do was re-interpret their meaning. In the past, I had understood these magnetic pulls as go-signals, prompting pedal-to-the-metal pursuits. Now, I began re-interpreting my electric attractions. No longer did they represent a go-signal, but instead, a flashing yellow light warning of possible danger, the equivalent of the Sirens in Greek mythology standing on rocky shoals, luring sailors to their deaths. That awareness and the memory of the pain these relationships inevitably wrought took the steam out of any desire for headlong pursuit. Now, whenever the siren songs of my attractions sounded, they clanged like a claxon in my head with much the same urgency one hears in old submarine warfare movies as the captain shouts into the com, "Dive! Dive! Dive!"

Over the months to follow, as I turned away from my magic attractions, they dissipated, though they never entirely disappeared. A choice now existed where previously none had been apparent. I was opting to maintain my sense of self by choosing not to lose myself in my *Imaginary Others*.

Much of the pain I have been through in my adult life has been self-inflicted. In this, I am not the exception but the rule. Of course, things happen to all of us that we cannot foresee. Even so, accepting that you are the author of your life may help you avoid some of the mistakes I have made. But frankly, I doubt it. We humans are driven to make whatever mistakes we *need* to make until we resolve the underlying issues that birthed those needs. Some may be able to do that alone, while others make use of psychotherapy.

Like most people, I am far happier sharing my life than alone. Having authentic and substantial feminine energy in my world adds to it immensely and helps complete me, but that is different than needing someone like a choking man who needs air. I alone am responsible for my happiness and fulfillment; no one else. Although things that are outside my control have and will be done to me, I am responsible for how I deal with them and the lessons I draw. After all, it is *my* life we are talking about; I alone must write my story and its meaning.

Of course, making such changes may sound daunting, and in some ways it is. However, the most daunting aspect is simply recognizing what is needed; that is what takes time. Once acceptance arrives, change often follows quickly.

CHAPTER 30

Dancing Her Dance

Mom was the yin to Dad's yang. Her domain was thoughtful conversations, evening walks, and nightly meditations called prayer. When visiting, I would join her on walks along the hard-packed dirt streets that crisscrossed Lake Monticello as the sun gave way to the moon and bright stars competed with the glow of fireflies. As we walked, we talked about God, my siblings, and what was going on in our lives. The song of crickets and the chorus of bullfrogs filled those nights, vying for dominance and threatening to drown out our conversation.

Throughout the years, Mom had grown while maintaining an active, caring presence, and when she had done what she could, she left the rest in the hands of her God. This had not always been the case. As the mother of twenty-somethings, she would stand firm against anything that broke her sense of righteousness. I remember her sputtering with indignation over what she saw as the impropriety of Jacques' wife, Christine, going out one night with her girlfriends while Jacques was in Vietnam. On another occasion, she took issue with how Christine raised her children, prompting Christine to order Mutti out of her home. Mutti was equally dogmatic when confronting Jane about pre-marital sex, essentially driving her away. And, when Ed told them he was marrying Ellen, of Philippine descent, Mutti and Dad cautioned against it, warning that Ed's life would be ruined.

However, in the following years, Mom mended these relationships, turning them into ones of mutual love and respect. Rather than remaining rigid, she flexed and became a more rounded and wiser person.

As with many mothers, Mom created the ground upon which the family rested and was the glue that held it together. She worried about the kids and took care of them, cooking, cleaning, and railing at us boys to clean our rooms and make our beds, only to follow behind to straighten the bedding to her exacting standards. She was also quite the character, donning a cowboy skirt and hat, corncob pipe in her mouth as she hammed it up in the kitchen, and cut a comical figure when trying to drive the geese from her yard by shooting them in the butt with a pellet gun from the upper deck.

Mom had grown more spiritual over the years, no longer governed by dogma but having her own thinking and beliefs on issues that troubled her vis-à-vis the church. Although she no longer marched in lockstep with church doctrine, she attended Mass every Sunday and knelt beside her bed every night for prayer. Her developing spirituality served her well in her living and her dying. She had become a whole person, no longer burdened by regrets as her life was nearing its end.

During her last two years, diagnosed with terminal cancer, Mutti lived her dying in a way beyond compare: with an unflinching grace made strong by her faith and a soulful conviction that she was returning to her God. Indeed, she made the process magnificent. I marveled how that was possible in the face of such dire tidings as she became ever more emaciated by radiation and chemotherapy treatments, lost all her hair, and endured frequent bouts of nausea. Yet, it was unmistakably true: with the passing of each day, and as her life grew closer to its end, she was becoming more of herself and at her pinnacle of beauty.

On two separate occasions, she did the most astonishing thing. She struggled out of bed one late evening while I sat with my siblings and their spouses around the dining room table. Teetering over, she placed her palms on the table for support and ignored everyone else. She leaned forward, looked me fiercely in the eye, and emphatically demanded in her French-accented English, "Charlie, have a *good* life! Charlie, have a *good* life!" She wasn't asking; she was telling. She then waited, unmoving, until, looking directly back into her eyes and choking back tears, I responded, "I will, Mom. I will." Without another word, she turned and tottered her frail, bent body back to bed.

Several months later, Mutti, even more sapped of energy, again made that arduous trek from her bed and repeated the very same words in the very same way. It seemed all-important to her to drive the point home, to drive the point *into* me, "Charlie, have a *good* life! Charlie, have a *good* life!"

I think she could see the dark ampule of my abandonment planted all those years ago and refused to leave me a second time. She was telling me that she *knew* with absolute conviction that it was within *my* power to move beyond it—if only I would. It was her blessing and dying wish for me; I took it to heart. Like a radioactive pellet inserted in the middle of a cancerous tumor, the directive to "Have a good life" became my goal.

My mother's love was not the perfect love I had wished for, and it was not always in a language I could appreciate. However, it was pure and honest love, only conveyed with increasing conviction by her emphatically challenging me to have a good life. By the time of her death, I knew that regardless of what had happened or why she had always loved me. With that absolute knowledge, she is forever with me.

My mother's peace with herself and her dying allowed her to keep her sense of humor and spirituality. Indeed, not only did these never flag, but they also burned ever brighter, even as cancer ravaged her body. Near the end, I took a picture of her and my daughter, Keeley, sitting together. Mutti's head was bare, her bald crown held erect, as she and Keeley stared resolutely into the camera's lens with their steady blue eyes. Two strong women, the younger channeling, the older. I wondered if they knew how alike they were.

Soon after this picture, Mutti laughingly showed me a note she had received from her best friend, Dot. In a beautiful flowing cursive, Dot wished her farewell and "Bon Voyage." *Christ!* I thought. *Now that's courage and class on the part of both these good and strong women.* Each of them faced death head-on. Mom's death would be within weeks, Dot's years later, but neither was afraid to meet it. For them, death was an accepted part of life, not separate from it.

In her final moments, as everyone was gathered around her death bed, Dad whispered to her, "You can let go, Madeleine. I'll be okay." With that, there was an audible escape of breath, and she was gone.

Madeleine Marie Alberta McCormack (nee Turgeon) passed away on February 20th, 1997, at age seventy-eight, and was buried at Arlington National Cemetery. The funeral services were conducted in North Post Chapel, Fort Myer, Virginia, where she and my father had married more than fifty years earlier.

CHAPTER 31

The Only Dance There Is

Near the end of his days, I remember Dad at the beach on Delaware Bay. Suffering from dementia, he sat hunched on the screened-in porch, hollowed out and shorn by age, scraggly legs protruding from his swimsuit like toothpicks from a withered olive. Facing the beauty of the bay, watching freighters making their way across, he repeatedly intoned in an awe-filled voice, "Is this for real? Is this for real?" As an aside, Mark expressed how sad it was that dad had come to this. Perplexed, I asked, "What are you talking about? Dad is a perfect example of addition by subtraction. He's a much nicer guy now than he's ever been." Mark considered this and then, with that sneer of a smile, said, "You know what? You're right!"

Many years ago, the philosopher, Ram Dass, wrote a book entitled: *The Only Dance There Is.* In it, he offered that people have a signature way of going through life that is only danced harder as life nears its end. I took this to heart as both a blessing and a warning. As Ram Dass had foretold, my mother lived her dying the way she had lived her living, only doing it better and better as the years went on. I cannot think of any more extraordinary gift a parent can give her children than the opportunity to witness an individual, a soul, continue to evolve until death lays its claim.

Dad also danced his dance and to a predictably different outcome: he withered. His dying years were marked by increasing frailty: strokes, dementia, Alzheimer's, alcoholism, hardening of the arteries, paranoia, fearfulness, and isolation, all mirroring his lifetime of self-devouring self-absorption. My parents' separate paths were not coincidental; each reflected the cumulative outcome of *how* they lived their lives.

The function of grief and mourning is to free the mourners to move on with their lives. Counter-intuitively, I believe grieving the loss of a genuinely connected relationship is more manageable than mourning a conflicted one. Like good milk, a fulfilling relationship is metabolized and internalized, becoming part of us and thus never lost. Conversely, a conflicted relationship is like sour milk: indigestible, remaining a foreign body that makes mourning difficult to complete. After all, how do you let go of someone important to you who has never been yours?

When Dad passed away, I was troubled by his loss but felt nothing like the acute pain of grief I had felt with my mother's death, which, though searing, passed quickly. With Dad, there was only the background hum of a general disquiet. Although gone from my life, he was a dreaded specter haunting my psyche.

That is until years later, while touring Florence, Italy, with my wife, Janet, we visited the US military cemetery. It had thousands of pearl-white gravestones gracing the rolling hillsides. The cemetery reminded me of one I saw with Dad when touring Italy as a boy; perhaps it was the same. As I walked alone among the monuments and those thousands upon thousands of graves, I wondered who these men and women had been, their stories, the lives they lived, the families they left behind, and their parents' long dead. In their twenties and thirties, these men and women had died seventy or more years earlier; I doubted many were alive who remembered them. I wondered if the meaning of their lives had been reduced to standing eternal guard as one of these gravestones, awesome to behold in their regimented multitude, but their individual stories lost forever.

I meandered among the graves for half an hour, musing upon such questions, when a daub of color caught my eye. In the distance, among all those thousands of graves, I spotted a single bouquet as if in answer to my unvoiced questions. Intrigued, I made my way to that grave and the fresh flowers carefully arranged by the headstone. It was the grave of a young man, a private killed in his early twenties.

Captured by the unknown story behind the flowers, I became lost in reverie. *Someone had recently visited this man and lovingly paid homage. Who could that have been, given that this man would have been at least ninety years old if he were alive today? Was it a girlfriend or a wife nearing the end of her life, still carrying the flame of her love? Was it a brother or sister who missed him terribly and still held him alive in memory? Was it a child, now nearly seventy years old, paying tribute to a father she had barely known—or not known at all?*

Those flowers, resting on that grave, were made even more poignant by the likelihood that whoever had left them, the holder of the private's memories, would be gone herself in a few short years. Then there would be no flowers nor anyone to hold his story. It would forever remain buried in the dark coffers below those well-tended lawns.

My musings kindled memories of times I'd lived with my parents. After all these years, the nostalgia finally slipped in, both sad and gently caressing, not for my mother but for my father. I thought of stories lived, stories told that, under the erosion of time, will be lost forever with no one left to leave a bouquet of memory. At first, my thoughts and feelings emerged as insubstantial as mirages, best seen from the corner of my eye. As I had discharged the effluvia of my anger toward Dad over the years, I now understood it had interfered with my ability to acknowledge the good he had brought into my life. As these memories slowly came into focus, I realized why I had needed to keep them as ghosts: despite all that was said and done, I missed those wild and wondrous moments that arose unexpectedly from time to time when in Dad's company.

It was morning. Dad called out: "Charlie, come with me; I want you to see something." We descended to the lakeshore, Dad carrying a tin can half-full of dried kernels of corn. A low-hanging fog cloaked the surface of the lake, its uppermost wisps cast in a golden halo by the early morning sun. As we stood on the shore, Dad began shaking the can, creating a sound like hard rain on a tin roof. Curiosity aroused, I waited silently and impatiently. Soon, a faint whisper arose in the distance and became a rhythmic whooshing of air that grew ever louder, its front approaching fast. A primal chill traversed my spine, an electric warning of what my mind had yet to grasp. Then, almost upon us, a wedge of geese, cawing like pre-historic beasts, burst from the fog. Just as I thought they had no time to stop, they, as one, broke their careening flight and splashed onto the water, turning it to a froth by the fury of their pulsating wings. With a contented, ill-concealed grin, Dad cast the corn upon the shore.

Of course, neither the neighbors nor my mother appreciated Dad's luring these poop factories into their yards, but, as usual, the feelings of others were like the writings of the Rosetta Stone to Dad: they did not translate. Nonetheless, I could understand his motivation. The pure, magnificently primitive power of that moment had called to my deepest nature.

Dad did one fatherly task exceptionally well: he introduced his kids to the excitement of the world. Dad carried us into various parts of Europe: Paris, Versailles, the Eiffel Tower, and the Louvre, where I saw the Mona Lisa for the first time. With him, we toured the Netherlands, visited Madurodam, where we walked like giants about the miniaturized city, and later drove by vast fields abloom with tulips as charming windmills slowly churned the air.

With him, we awoke to continental breakfasts of meats and cheeses, butter and jellies, and bread of all kinds. We traversed the snow-capped Alps, our car laboring up steep inclines as we looked out at villages, miniaturized by the enormity of the mountains, which dotted shadowed valleys and sun-lit mountainsides alike.

With him, we camped at Lake Garda, Italy, settled in a family-sized tent that Dad taught us to erect out of a confusing mélange of canvas and aluminum rods. There, he took us on a powerboat ride, skimming across the swells as our eyes blazed with excitement and our hearts filled with exhilaration every time the spray of wind-blown water anointed our faces.

Dad, a history buff, led us on a fantastic tour of Italy. His stories brought the ancient buildings and cities to life and took us hundreds and thousands of years back in time as we crossed the remnants of old Roman roads and crumbling viaducts plunging down steep mountainsides.

Dad fought in WWII in Italy. He told us of Mussolini and how he got the trains to run on time, and he showed us the balcony from which an angry mob hung Mussolini at the war's end. As we traversed the route of his military campaign, from one end of Italy to the other, Dad recounted his stories as a young artillery officer. Upon a curving mountain road, a sniper's bullet had just missed him as he drove in a jeep. On a hilltop, Dad fell into a trench latrine when a German artillery round exploded nearby. And, from a hillside overlooking an open field bracketed by dense woods, he recreated the tension and disbelief he felt when a German infantry battalion, oblivious to the danger, emerged from the forest below. As the Germans approached the center of the field, farthest from the safety of the woods, his canon opened fire and obliterated them.

Amazingly, we also stopped at a hilltop manor that Dad said was the home of a girlfriend of that time. He knocked on the door, and an attractive, dignified middle-aged woman answered. Dad introduced himself, and with surprised delight, she gave him a warm hug and a kiss.

I marveled at Dad's capacity to navigate across Europe and through the narrow streets of the Italian cities with a map alone. My respect would only grow more profound when I repeatedly get lost, even with the benefit of GPS, some forty-five years later. We drove into Venice, where we watched Murano glassmakers work their art and rode in a Gondola. Then we moved to the wonders of Rome: the Vatican and the Colosseum, where Dad could not miss the opportunity to spin his tales and weave new worlds into our imaginings.

He explained the symbolism of the sculptures in various squares and within the many fountains dotting the city. He also purchased indulgences for each of us that supposedly guaranteed we could bypass the trials of Purgatory and gain direct access to heaven upon our deaths.

With Dad, we toured the United States, going to many places I would return to years later in my trip with Jane and to which I would subsequently take my kids: The Grand Canyon, the Painted Desert, and the Petrified Forest. We also rode ponies in Colorado and had our picture taken near bison. All this we owed to Dad, and now, with him long gone and tears flooding my eyes, I could finally find my way to thank him.

Passing through and seeing past my anger allowed me to remember the good times with Dad and find compassion for him. I was finally free to mourn. In reconciling myself with him in this complete way, I let go of his oppressive hold upon me and became more open to moving on freely with my life.

John Crisler McCormack died on September 4th, 2003, at age eighty-five. He was buried on a rainy day at Arlington National Cemetery with full military honors, casket pulled on a caisson, followed by the honor guard led by a riderless horse, empty boot facing backward in the stirrup. At the gravesite, a bagpiper played "Amazing Grace," followed by a bugler sounding out the hauntingly beautiful last twenty-four notes of taps. The sharp clap of three rifle volleys rang out in final salute and farewell; silence flooded into the ensuing void.

Wherever he is, whatever form he is in, I only wish him well.

CHAPTER 32

Real Relationship

Last night I had a dream. Janet and I were in a large open kitchen, Janet gowned in a colorful dress. Her head thrown back, eyes alight, laughing without restraint, dancing to music only she could hear. Twirling round and round, she moves toward me, then away, in silent invitation. I can hear the music of her laughter and the beat of her Riverdance steps, and I cannot help but respond. Slowly beginning my spin, moving toward her, then away, we weave a tapestry of coming together and then moving apart but never touching. The intensity builds, then ebbs then returns to ever higher plateaus. Joy.

In the last quarter of my life, I am in another love story. This one has a distinctly different quality, somewhat like the atmospheric change one experiences in moving from the glare and heat of an unremitting sun to the shade of an oak tree under which stands two chairs, a table, and a cold pitcher of Sangria. Unlike my previous romantic relationships, this story is neither dramatic nor eventful, and I love it that way.

Janet and I met on a social website. What attracted me, besides her appearance, was her plain-spoken profile. She had a good job, owned a home, and raised two boys, all while obtaining a master's degree. These characteristics suggested a strong work ethic, strength of character, courage, the capacity to persevere, independence, intelligence, and a well-established personhood.

I emailed her, then gulped when she immediately suggested we talk on the phone. I called and swallowed hard again when she proposed we meet in person. Already Friday night, I suggested the following weekend. She demurred; she had plans. I suggested the weekend following that. Again, she balked, noting that is a long time off. I was confused; w*hat's left?* The only time I could think of was the next night. Without hesitation, she chirped, "That works fine," as if it had been my idea.

I knocked on the door of her split-level brick and aluminum-sided house in a middle-class neighborhood. The door opened, revealing Janet bent over, struggling to keep her cat from escaping. She tilted her head up and, struck by the humor of that awkward greeting, offered a smile that threatened to give way to laughter. Along with the warmth of her spirit resided the radiance of her frankly appraising eyes: one brown, the other green, both offering the warm welcome of a winter's fire.

We closed an Italian restaurant that evening, not dancing the fandango but in animated conversation. I watched her, looking for pretense or a vain woman's wiles. But with Janet, what you see is what you get. I was not dumbstruck or infatuated, just relaxed and with an unexpected feeling of being at home. This was a welcome relief, given the mind-frying electric overloads of previous relationships. Subsequently, we spent nearly every weekend together: talking, cooking, slow dancing, and eventually making love.

Some might say that Janet sounds like the safe choice for someone who now finds passion too risky. Perhaps they are right; I do not know how to gauge that. What I do *know* is that with Janet, I experience a lasting contentment that is well beyond any I have known. While other relationships offered intermittent spikes of ecstasy, they also included stomach-tightening troughs of enmity, and none has come close to raising the floor of secure connection and contentment that I experience daily with Janet.

Healthy relationships are fluid: forming and reforming like a vase rising on the potter's wheel. The vase of relationship requires two potters working with each other. Successful potters of relationships understand that they must consider the needs of the other without necessarily relinquishing their own. It is important that neither covertly harbors resentment over the eventual outcome. If they do not learn to work together in a mutually reciprocal relationship, the vase will become misshapen and prone to breakage. Many do not appreciate that this interpersonal process of thesis, antithesis, and synthesis constitutes the vital core of the relationship itself.

I have come to understand that power and relationship stand in inverse association with one another in romantic relationships. The more one or the other partner relies on power to have their way, the less genuine the relationship. Just think about it. The root of the word relationship is *relate*, not *dominate.* It is only in authentic relating that we achieve secure connection and intimacy.

Counter-intuitively, although intimacy is much vaunted, most people fear it. Why? Because it entails the *will toward vulnerability*. That is, the willingness of each partner to be transparent and to share their thoughts and feelings without blame, shame, attack, or demand for change. Intimacy's only goal is to reveal one's inner workings to the other, not to change the other. It aims at deepening understanding and connection. Blaming, shaming, attacking, or demanding runs counter to this aim, introducing threats, undermining the sense of safety, and consequently inhibiting the willingness to communicate. In a relationship where one person wins, both lose.

Consequently, intimacy is the road to deepening connection when it meets with good results (bilateral intimacy) and increasing emotional divorce when it does not. It takes two to make a relationship work, only one to destroy it.

Janet's ability to be herself, her strength of character, her personhood, and her unwillingness to be pushed from a point of view if the shift is not genuine thrills me. She is straightforward, willing to confront me when unhappy with what I am doing, and genuinely takes to heart what I have to say when I am concerned by something. These simple traits fill me with an exquisite feeling of love and being loved that has a tensile strength unlike any other I have known.

Janet also brings to the relationship her remarkable capacity to enjoy ordinary things: seasonal decorating, cooking, and spontaneous hugs and kisses.

I am astonished by her generosity of spirit and personal integrity, as well as her capacity to speak her mind, but rarely nastily. She never talks the talk; she only walks the walk without fanfare or self-promotion. She inhabits herself, her world, and her relationships, providing a secure and loving connection I have always wanted. She gives me that special place called home.

Importantly, Janet is game for going on my occasional adventures. Before we were married, she went with me, my daughters, and son-in-law Jason for a ten-day sailing vacation around the Greek Isles. I hired a boat and captain, so on the cheap that I had concerns about the seaworthiness of both. The trip was wonderful. We laugh when remembering Captain George loudly announcing at 9 am each morning that it was "Beer-O'clock!" as he cracked his first beer of the day and how he would hoot while telling the tale of an English gentleman who, when the cocktail hour arrived, would announce, "It's time for a stiffy." We smile when remembering Jason's newly discovered love of goat meat, warranting the nickname: The Goat Hunter. And sympathize as we recall Cait bursting into tears when at a shack of a restaurant on an isolated Greek island, we so entertained the owner that he plopped a liver, dripping with its jellies, upon the table as a gift, proudly proclaiming he had just cut it from a baby goat.

But the most treasured memory occurred on the trip over. Janet and I had a seven-hour layover in Athens and caught a cab to what I promised was a renowned restaurant. The taxi dropped us off in a narrow, crowded alleyway of a street humming with commerce, where merchants hung colorful garments and adorn makeshift shelves with items for sale. There was no restaurant to be found at the address, only a jewelry store. Janet asked, "Where's the restaurant?" Professing confusion, I commented, "It must be around here somewhere," while watching Janet's eyes inexorably drawn to the sparkling store window. After a few minutes, her face alight looking at the bright objects, the restaurant momentarily forgotten, I whisper in her ear, "While you're looking, why don't you pick out a wedding ring?" Her radiant smile was all for me.

On a more recent adventure, Janet overcame her trepidation to go along with my desire to rent a trawler in Sarasota, Florida. I wanted to see if I liked cruising the intercoastal waterway; I was considering cruising the Great Loop. Several days into our excursion, a sudden squall hammered us with rain and wind so violent that visibility dropped to near zero. As the boat rocked and swung about in the storm, life sprung one of its little surprises: the windlass (the automatic anchor release mechanism) failed. We watched helplessly as the anchor and 1500 feet of chain were lost overboard. Without the stabilizing powers of the anchor, our 25,000-pound trawler whipped around like a miniature toy before running aground. I was mainly relieved that we had not blindly run into another boat.

As the storm passed, we found ourselves some distance from where we had been, facing 180 degrees in the opposite direction, grounded on a sandbar, and beginning to roll, not knowing if or when it would stop. Finally, it settled on a twenty-five-degree angle, spilling gallons of diesel fuel into the cabin. Driven out by fumes and worried about fire, we spent the night on deck, feet propped against railings to prevent us from sliding overboard. That was enough for Janet to nix any idea of traveling the Great Loop.

In my relationship with Janet, now twelve years and nine grandchildren long, our willingness to be intimate meets with consistently good results, and our connection grows. Rather than having *fallen in love* with all the fire of Halley's comet, we continue to *ascend to love* in a slow, steady climb talking, laughing, and occasionally crying, mostly in joy but sometimes in sorrow too.

Recently, Janet looked over at me, eyes welling with tears, and said, "Charlie, I'm so happy with my life, and that mainly has to do with you. Thank you. I love you." At that, she was not the only person with tears in her eyes.

CHAPTER 33

Au Revoir

Now, all these years later, as I gaze out upon the incomparable beauty of the Bush River, I imagine each of you with my mind's eye. Many of you have left home and created lives and families of your own, while others are new to the fold, your lives just beginning. I also see the many patients, my fellow travelers, who have honored me over the years by allowing me into their lives, thereby adding immeasurably to my own. And I see others still, strangers who are not strangers at all, who have stumbled upon this work and recognize a part of themselves in my story and a part of me in theirs.

For my part, clearing seventy, I try to pare the "to-do" list of daily life and obligations to essentials, enjoying the oscillating interplay of being with others and the luxury of being with myself. Janet is about, but we each do our own thing during the day, coming together for cards, TV, and dinner in the evening or for boat rides and the occasional trip. Over the years, I have come to appreciate how much love and the acceptance of separateness and difference go together.

Now, partially retired, I can generally do what I want when I want—an oddly disconcerting experience after years of maintaining stimulating identities as friend, father, therapist, author, lecturer, and mate. Although it may seem somewhat inane, I continue to ask myself, *Who am I now? Who am I becoming? Who do I want to become?*

I am not one who wants to kill time by going through the motions or staying busy for busy's sake. I call on myself to be patient, to take one step at a time, to *be* with myself then to *go on being* with myself until I figure out where my being is going. In this way, I try to make space for whatever might emerge from within me.

Now, through the course of a day, I move from seeing a few patients to reading to picking up a guitar, to writing, swimming, or boating with Janet, finding joy in the swooping seagulls that follow our wake in shallow flight. I sit in the sunroom listening to the river lapping against the beach as the leaves of the ancient oaks whisper secrets long forgotten. I watch squirrels irreverently chatter and scramble up tree trunks as birds chirp and squawk. I watch geese moving along the sandy beach below my house and smile in memory at the shenanigans of Mom and Dad, now fully appreciating the problem of poop. I listen to the wind and, on those rainy days, the thrumming of the raindrops on the windowpane. All these sounds intone in the deep background of my consciousness, quieting the ghosts of decades past in a language that, like the sound of ocean waves breaking upon the beach or the rhythmic beating of a mother's heart, soothes the soul.

I look forward to visiting with my grandkids, watching the joy that lights their faces when they see me, only equaled, if not surpassed, by my delight in seeing and playing with them. But soon, tired, body aching, and mind restless with the need for adult engagements, I am glad to get back to my more solitary pursuits.

Luckily, through the years, Jane and I have continued to celebrate our kids' milestone events together, inclusive of current spouses and extended family. These are beautiful occasions, forever healing across time. Just the other day, we were both at Keeley's house, Jane rocking Caitlin's two-year-old son, Ryan, in a chair while I paced about holding Quincy, Keeley's three-month-old, in my arms. Jane gently called my name. I turned to see Ryan in her arms, raising his right arm straight up alongside his head and then flipping his hand like a periscope, giving me his signature wave: he was starting to warm to me. Jane smiled her tender smile, and I smiled back.

I question myself from time to time, *Am I in the most secure position, or one from which I am guaranteed to fall? Am I in mid-leap, letting go of over-used and obsolete senses of self in search of emerging ones?* Sometimes, I know the answer. Sometimes, I do not.

I think about how far I have come from those early traumas and failures. In trying to understand myself, I remember that I used to ask one question at each psychoanalytic conference, hoping that these world-class thinkers could light the way, "What makes the difference between those who fall and can't get up and those who do get up and go on to live meaningful lives?" I never did receive a satisfying answer. Then one night, while going through a book of art, I happened upon a picture of a seventeenth-century American Indian shaman with the following caption:

"What I am trying to say is hard to tell and hard to understand...
unless, unless...
you have been yourself at the edge of the Deep Canyon and have come back unharmed.
Maybe it all depends on something within yourself—
whether you are trying to see the Watersnake or the sacred Cornflower,
whether you go out to meet death or to Seek Life."
Shaman: The Paintings of Susan Seddon Boulet (1989)

Those words resonated within me: it depends on what you are looking for. Are *you* looking for life or death? Are *you* looking for love or hate? Are *you* engaged in a continual re-working of the unchangeable past or striving to create a new day and better future? Are *you* looking to play the music of your life like yourself, composing new melodies, or like that of your childhood, marching lockstep with your parents and their parents and the generations that came before? The Indian shaman and the Bible agree, "Seek, and ye shall find."

Now, it is time for me to embark on my solo trip to Norfolk, Virginia, on my 25' deck boat: *Enchanted.* Norfolk is 180 nautical miles away, a 360-mile roundtrip: I feel a need to push myself again, to return to the edge of my comfort zone. To get out of my head and into the moment. I have never done anything like *this* before, but I need to clear the cobwebs that are beginning to bind, and there is nothing like a Great Adventure to do that.

I could not find anyone crazy enough to go along with me, so I am going alone. That turned out for the best; I hungered to be alone with myself. My main worry is that there are parts of the journey where land is not visible, and radio and cell phone reception are unavailable. I ask myself, "What happens if the engine throws a belt or one of the Chesapeake Bay's infamous thunderstorms catches me?" I know what a squall can do to a twenty-five-thousand-pound trawler. What it could do to my thirty-five-hundred-pound deck boat is anyone's guess.

Ah! These worries, these risks, are not to be avoided; they *are* the point. The challenge they represent sharpens my thinking. Depending upon sea and weather conditions, the trip could take anywhere from eight to eighteen hours or not be completed at all. I buy a spotlight in case I'm stuck on the water after dark, double-check the safety equipment, and scour marine weather forecasts, wave heights and frequency, currents, wind speed, and direction predictions. Anything less will be a suicidal wish. What better way to clear the mind than dancing with Mother Nature? It all looks good, but marine forecasts can be as wrong as any other and given to sudden change.

The night before my trip, I stood alone at the end of the pier. The sun had set long ago, its rays now traveling so far around the world they barely blush the edge of the night. A quarter moon graces the black-felt sky, framed by five glimmering stars rendering jeweled elegance as Rosetta color slivers the skyline. Pilings stand tall, casting dark shadows upon the deep water—itself eerily still as if waiting to draw a breath. Canadian Geese caw, unseen in the distance, as they prepare for their winter migration. The pre-historic black profile of a blue heron soundlessly cuts the night in front of my eyes. I fill with gratitude.

At 6:15 a.m. the following day, Janet walks me to the boat. We hug our farewells with tearful eyes and my heart in my throat. I start the engine, put the boat in gear, and cruise slowly away from Janet, from home. I wonder if *this* will be the *last of things* as I travel toward the rising sun.

I feel so alive!

I hear my mother's voice faintly calling in the distance—

"Charlie, have a good life! Charlie, have a good life!"

And I hear Aunt Dot's voice echoing down through the years—

"Bon Voyage!"

ACKNOWLEDGMENTS

This book began as the story of my life's journey but soon became the journey itself. After completing each edition, I would feel satisfied, only for that feeling to fade several months later when I re-read the manuscript with fresh eyes or when the truth of someone's critical review resonated with me.

Along this arduous process, many have contributed. Friends and family read part of the early manuscript and others the whole; some provided feedback while others kept their counsel. I thank them all; even silence tells a story.

Then there was The Golden Few, who resonated with the work and rose to meet it. My daughter Keeley, a psychotherapist herself, responded enthusiastically, while conversely, my daughter Caitlin, an accountant, was uninterested in psychological teachings while unabashedly challenging me to create a good read.

Mark and Carol Ann, my youngest brother and sister-in-law, bubbled with excitement. At one point, Mark, sensing my dispirited demeanor from some tepid feedback, wrote, "Don't let the bastards get you down. It's good. I never lost interest." In truth, there were no bastards, and it wasn't all that good, only the first of countless revisions to follow.

In a poignant letter, my sister, Michelle, made me aware of how my memories had rekindled her own and re-enveloped her in mourning. Writing from her memories as a fifteen-year-old girl, Michelle supplied a glimpse into the human underbelly of my parents, resurrecting those times in a way that only a young girl can.

Patricia Alfin, LCSW-C, a former supervisee, brought my first published work to the attention of the Washington School of Psychiatry, thereby altering the course of my life. Also, having quickly gone through the manuscript, she saw where the book was going before it had arrived and offered valuable suggestions.

Jason Thomas, my African American son-in-law, brought greater racial sensitivity to my writing. At the same time, my friend Wayne "Killer" Kirgel dove in and edited it without my having to ask.

During the writing of my first book, Treating Borderline States in Marriage: Dealing with Oppositionalism, Ruthless Aggression, and Severe Resistance (Jason Aronson, 2000), I leaned heavily on my friend, Ron Zuskin (The Z-Man): a psychotherapist, raconteur, social work educator, musician, and gifted songwriter; Ron shines with intelligence and creativity. We first met professionally and at once bonded. With my first book, we created a synergy that powered me through the painstaking process. This time, unfortunately, fate conspired so that it may not be so; Ron was ill and unavailable. However, I had lost one support only to find another when Wayne Kirgel arrived.

Well acquainted with life's challenges, Ron would later rise from his sickbed. With his usual generosity of time, talent, and grace, he edited a later version of the original manuscript, humoring, cajoling, and haranguing me to make the book more alive. He was never happy with it, always insisting I write it as a Hero's Journey, but, as I was to learn, telling me this was one thing, showing me how, as editor Iris Marsh did, was quite another.

Then there's Jane, my first wife and the mother of our three children, to whom I had been married for eighteen years. Initially, I refused to write about our relationship. Jane had suffered a psychiatric illness, and I feared rekindling those difficult times. Still, my editor of that early version, Margaret Diehl, insisted that the tale would be depersonalized with the surface handling of my relationship with Jane rather than given flesh and bone, with a breath and heartbeat of its own. Finally, after much trepidation, I wrote the chapter on our relationship. I emailed it to Jane along with a message confessing my unease and giving her full veto power over that section of the manuscript. After I suffered days of skittering angst and nights of troubled sleep, fearing I had upset Jane, she responded. Not only did she approve of the chapter, but she asked that I not change a word, feeling that it was "beautifully written" and that "your care for me shines through." Heart swelling, tears coursed my face as I filled with gratitude and relief, transformed by her bountifully affirming words.

There is also Janet, my third wife, who provided enormous amounts of uninterrupted time for writing and her characteristically honest feedback at a moment's notice.

Not to be left out was my second editor Jacob Wakesa, a twenty-nine-year-old medical student and recently married Kenyan, who graduated from Oxford with a degree in literature. He and I entered a creative collaboration that soon became a friendship. Unfortunately, Jacob contracted Covid-19 and was hospitalized for months, only to later suffer "long-haul" complications requiring surgery. It was no longer possible for him to work on the book.

I then recruited Irish Marsh, a native of the Netherlands and a gifted developmental editor. She dove right to the heart of the problem, eliminating 20,000 words, and re-ordering sections via cut and paste, to give a smoother flow and more power to the writing. She taught me the difference between "showing" and "telling" and to stay on message, facilitating decisions about which stories to keep and which to jettison.

Then, once I thought all the help I was going to get had been got, an angel came into my life: Christine L. Terrell, MD, a specialist in infectious diseases. Some time ago, she responded on the Goodreads website to my request for Beta Readers. After significant delays caused by my ineptitude, she finally received the manuscript and, some days later, responded. She had gone through the entire text, calling out typos and making important suggestions to improve the reading. But as importantly, she wrote about her thoughts and the various aspects of the writing that had both stimulated her thinking and moved her heart. Hers was such a generous missive that I showed it to Janet, who read it twice before responding in one word with a smile that gave way to happy laughter: “Wow!”

What do you call such people, some of whom enter our lives serendipitously but nonetheless add so much to them with their generosity? Oh. I know. Friends. Not to say that others are not, for they are, but these were The Golden Few. May they always remain beacons to those around them.

Charlie.

Note to the reader: Thank you for reading *Healing of a Psychotherapist,* Please take a moment to share your experience with others by submitting a review. If you wish to contact me directly, email me: **charlesmccormack81@gmail.com.**

With heartfelt thanks,

Charles McCormack

About the Author

Charles McCormack MA, MSW, LCSW-C, a Clinical Social Worker of the Year in the state of Maryland and the author of several publications, including ***Treating Borderline States in Marriage: Dealing with Oppositionalism, Ruthless Aggression*** and ***Severe Resistance,*** holds master's degrees in Psychology and Clinical Social Work. In 1988 McCormack became the Senior Social Worker of Adult Long-term Inpatient Services at the Sheppard-Pratt Psychiatric Hospital in Baltimore, supervising social workers on seven units covering 140 inpatients. He has also worked in drug treatment, psychiatric day and evening hospitals, a Baltimore inner-city family violence clinic, and sexual abuse treatment programs.

In 1989, McCormack authored the paper ***The Borderline/Schizoid Marriage: The Holding Environment as an Essential Treatment Construct***, translating lessons learned in inpatient care to outpatient practice, which led to his being invited to speak at the Washington School of Psychiatry and subsequently to join the faculty.

In 2006 McCormack graduated from The New Directions Writing from a Psychoanalytic Perspective program of the Washington Center for Psychoanalysis. In 2016 he began writing the first of three editions of ***Hatching Charlie***, a finalist in several international book contests in the categories of self-help, inspirational, and psychology. Forever learning and evolving as a writer, McCormack rewrote ***Hatching Charlie*** into ***Essence***, the 2022 winner of the Montaigne Medal, as the most thought-provoking book under the umbrella of the Eric Hoffer Book Award. In 2023 McCormack rewrote ***Essence*** into ***Healing of a Psychotherapist***, to capture the personal struggles we all have as human beings striving to become ever better versions of ourselves.

Today, McCormack resides on the shores of the Bush River in Aberdeen, Maryland, just off the Chesapeake Bay, where he maintains a small private practice and pursues photography, boating, hosting his nine grandchildren, and thinking about life, relationships, and the challenges of the aging process.

Ingram Content Group UK Ltd.
Milton Keynes UK
UKHW020657240723
425668UK00014B/722